"The word *wonderful* is a cliché these days, meaning simply 'very good.' This book, though, reclaims what it means to be wonder-full. Mike Cosper, one of the keenest gospel Christian analysts of culture alive today, shows us in this book why our world has become so disenchanted and charts us back to the joy of awe. This is an awe-full and wonder-full book, in the right meaning of both of those words."
Russell Moore, president, Ethics and Religious Liberty Commission of the Southern Baptist Convention

"Do we need another book on classical disciplines of the Christian life? I have read many, but *Recapturing the Wonder* reads differently. It is a deeply spiritual, easily accessible, and creatively written book that encouraged my heart and exposed some disenchantment in the crevices of my own soul. I'll be handing this book out quite a bit. If you feel a little dry and disillusioned or need a refresher on God's invitation to know him more deeply through the practice of the disciplines, this book will serve you well."
Matt Chandler, lead teaching pastor, The Village Church

"*Recapturing the Wonder* pulls you in from the first story of a tomcat catching a raccoon and keeps you reading until the final challenge to live the good life. You will love it. Mike Cosper has a way of expressing what we are all feeling and experiencing, and he makes sense of it all. He knows our deepest questions and innermost yearnings and creatively points to Jesus for all the answers."
Kyle Idleman, author of *Not a Fan* and *Grace is Greater*

"Am I ever simply where I am or is my mind constantly somewhere else? Am I able to sit in silence and enjoy the ambient noise or must I always be looking at my phone? These were some of the convicting questions I found myself asking as I read Mike Cosper's book *Recapturing the Wonder*. Reading his book caused my heart to long for more of Jesus, more rest in him, and more time with him, not to earn his favor but because of who he is. Find time to sit and read Cosper's rich and practical book. You'll be glad you did."
Trillia Newbell, author of *Enjoy, Fear and Faith*, and *United*

"The sieve of modern skepticism has drained some of the richest substance from belief; we and the world are all the poo
Wonder guides us toward a re-enchanted Ch
pelling, convicting, and, well, *enchanting*. Th
Karen Swallow Prior, author of *Booked* and *Fier*

"Disenchantment, cynicism, and skepticism are ubiquitous in our present time. We still long for wonder, but we seek it apart from the Wonderful One. In *Recapturing the Wonder*, Mike Cosper takes us by the hand, inviting us to relinquish our jadedness by receiving the wonder found in the gospel of Jesus Christ."

Ekemini Uwan, writer and speaker

"*Recapturing the Wonder* is a winsome wake-up call, calling us back to ourselves and back to God. It's conversational and straightforward, full of heart and authenticity. Through simple spiritual practices freshly applied, Cosper invites us to practice the integration of grace against the disconnect of this modern life."

Sandra McCracken, singer and songwriter

RECAPTURING THE
WONDER

———

TRANSCENDENT FAITH IN

A DISENCHANTED WORLD

MIKE COSPER

IVP Books

An imprint of InterVarsity Press
Downers Grove, Illinois

InterVarsity Press
P.O. Box 1400, Downers Grove, IL 60515-1426
ivpress.com
email@ivpress.com

InterVarsity Press® is the book-publishing division of InterVarsity Christian Fellowship/USA®, a movement of students and faculty active on campus at hundreds of universities, colleges, and schools of nursing in the United States of America, and a member movement of the International Fellowship of Evangelical Students. For information about local and regional activities, visit intervarsity.org.

Scripture quotations, unless otherwise noted, are from The Holy Bible, English Standard Version, copyright © 2001 by Crossway Bibles, a division of Good News Publishers. Used by permission. All rights reserved.

While any stories in this book are true, some names and identifying information may have been changed to protect the privacy of individuals.

Published in association with the literary agent Don Gates of The Gates Group, www.the-gates-group.com.

Cover design: David Fassett
Interior design: Jeanna Wiggins
Images: © 472845096/iStockphoto

ISBN 978-0-8308-4506-4 (print)
ISBN 978-0-8308-9076-7 (digital)

Printed in the United States of America ∞

Library of Congress Cataloging-in-Publication Data
Names: Cosper, Mike, 1980- author.
Title: Recapturing the wonder: transcendent faith in a disenchanted world /
*   Mike Cosper.*
Description: Downers Grove: InterVarsity Press, 2017. | Includes
*   bibliographical references.*
Identifiers: LCCN 2017022343 (print) | LCCN 2017019245 (ebook) | ISBN
*   9780830890767 (eBook) | ISBN 9780830845064 (pbk. : alk. paper)*
Subjects: LCSH: Spiritual life--Christianity. | Christian life.
Classification: LCC BV4501.3 (print) | LCC BV4501.3 .C688 2017 (ebook) | DDC
*   248.4--dc23*
LC record available at https://lccn.loc.gov/2017022343

P	21	20	19	18	17	16	15	14	13	12	11	10	9	8	7	6	5	4	3	2	1
Y	34	33	32	31	30	29	28	27	26	25	24	23	22	21	20	19	18	17

For Dorothy and Maggie:

Here's hoping this book helps you

make sense of this strange world.

For Mike Frazier and Rich Plass,

who helped make sense of this world for me.

Contents

Introduction   1

1 Discovering Our Disenchantment   7
   Pathway One: Re-Enchanting Our World 27

2 Modern Religious Sacrifices
   and the God Who Ends Religion 33
   Pathway Two: Experiencing Grace 49

3 Selfie Sticks, Spectacles, and Sepulchers 53
   Pathway Three: Bringing Scripture to Life 69

4 Solitude and Secrecy 74
   Pathway Four: Withdrawing With God 85

5 Abundance and Scarcity 89
   Pathway Five: Practicing Abundance 104

6 Feasts of Attention 109
   Pathway Six: Throwing a Feast 131

7 The Monastery and the Road 136
   Pathway Seven: The Rule of Life 151

Epilogue: One Final Wonder 159

Acknowledgments 165

Notes 167

Introduction

When I was a kid, I had a semi-feral tomcat that was fond of leaving animal carcasses on our front step. He was huge and grey and had long, matted fur. I'd be on my way to school and open the door to find him waiting, a bird or a squirrel or a small rabbit—often headless, by this time—in his mouth or at his feet, a look of self-satisfied pride in his eyes.

One morning, I found him with the carcass of a raccoon not much smaller than he was. The cat didn't look much better than the raccoon. His ear was torn and bleeding, and patches of fur were missing from all over his body, which was punctuated by scratches and tooth marks. I vaguely remember him missing a tooth, too. But that same dark look of pride was in his eyes.

I imagined what led to that scene, something akin to a bar fight gone horribly wrong, leading him to come to his friend in the early dawn and ask for help burying the body. I got a shovel and we got rid of the raccoon together.

I feel like that cat looking over the pages of this manuscript. I set out to write a book about spiritual disciplines—practices like Scripture reading and prayer and fasting—and found myself in the midst of a fight that, like the cat, I was unprepared for. I knew I wanted to account for what makes those habits so difficult to cultivate, so elusive. I didn't know how much I'd have to reckon with a world that conditions us for doubt. Most of all, I didn't know how much I'd have to reckon with my own doubts.

At the same time, the disciplines became more important to me than ever. In the two-and-a-half years that passed between writing a proposal for this book and actually finishing it, life has been chaotic. I witnessed the meltdown of several close friends' marriages, the church where I served as a pastor went through several difficult transitions, and my family went through bouts of severe illness. Everything seemed to ratchet up the pressure, and at times, my only lifeline and grip on sanity was these disciplines. I write about them not as a master of the many methods and techniques that have been employed throughout church history but as someone who has found that they can be an anchor for faith, hope, and love in the midst of a life that feels like it's crumbling.

But the disciplines didn't just provide the strength to endure the troubles that this world threw at me; they opened up the possibility of living in another world.

In Susanna Clarke's wonderful fairytale *Jonathan Strange and Mr. Norrell*, she tells a story about the rediscovery of magic in England in the nineteenth century. In the beginning of the tale, magic has vanished from England. It remains part of English folklore, like the story of King Arthur, but no one has actually practiced it in many years. Nonetheless, there were men who called themselves magicians. They did so in spite of the fact that "not one of these magicians had ever cast the smallest spell, nor by magic caused one leaf to tremble upon a tree, made one mote of dust to alter its course or changed a single hair upon any one's head. But with this one minor reservation, they enjoyed a reputation as some of the wisest and most magical gentlemen in Yorkshire."[1]

These magicians spent their days in lengthy arguments about theoretical magic, debating the use of this spell over that, nitpicking the details of magic's history in England, meeting once a month and reading "long, dull papers" to one another. The idea of actually practicing magic was vulgar.

Then Mr. Norrell showed up. He cast a spell that made all of the statues in Yorkshire's cathedral come to life: shouting, singing, and telling stories about the deaths of the men and women whose images they bore. The magicians of Yorkshire were speechless. The world was far different than they'd believed.

I couldn't help but feel a certain sadness reading *Jonathan Strange and Mr. Norrell*. I found myself identifying with the magicians of Yorkshire. My life as a Christian had left me with a certain amount of fluency with faith: I could keep up in conversations about theology, the history of the Bible, the world of the first century, and the history of the church. I could talk a bit about apologetics and worldview. And I could talk a good bit about worship and liturgy in the church. But as I read Clarke's book, I couldn't help but feel the gap between knowing and know-how, between what I knew I could *say* about my faith and what I could *do* with it. At times, my faith felt like a boxed-in corner of my life, separate and distinct from the rest of it.

Strangely, this isn't because of a lack of events in my life that could be called miraculous. In fact, I've seen more than a few things that I can't explain rationally, and I've had spiritual experiences that felt no less than spectacular. But these, too, felt somehow boxed-in, an island I occasionally took a ferry to, rather than the mainland of my everyday experience. Even the little things that make up a "Christian" life—going to church, reading the Bible, and so on—felt tacked on and disconnected from the rest of my life. My ordinary life felt strangely irreligious.

⁓

Much of this book is an attempt to understand why such a gap exists and what we might do about it. It's an attempt to sketch out the spiritual landscape of an age that has been called a "secular age," an "age of anxiety," and a "culture of narcissism,"[2] and an effort at finding a path into a different way of life.

Transformation is a before-and-after story, and to know what the after looks like (and how to get there), it's necessary to have a sense of the before. For most Christians, our before picture is shaped by decades of immersion in this strange world and strange culture that surrounds us. It's had a deep and powerful formative effect on us.

This is an age where our sense of spiritual possibility, transcendence, and the presence of God has been drained out. What's left is a spiritual desert, and Christians face the temptation to accept the dryness of that desert as the only possible world. We have enough conviction and faith to be able to call ourselves believers, but we're compelled to look for ways to live out a Christian life without transcendence and without the active presence of God, practicing what Dallas Willard once called "biblical deism"—a strange bastardization of Christianity that acts as though, once the Bible was written, God left us to sort things out for ourselves.

In such a world, the Bible feels like a dead text and our prayers seem to bounce answerless off the drywall. Practicing our faith feels more fruitless than talking about it, and we end up very much like the magicians of Yorkshire, able to talk fluently about magic and almost certain that it doesn't exist. The practical magic that's missing isn't just the dramatic—healing the sick or raising the dead. Rather, it's the more quiet and invisible magic of how anxious souls find wholeness and how broken people find healing. We might be fluent in the language of faith but unable to pray, overwhelmed by fear and anxiety, and victim to the compulsive, distracting habits that fill our age. We might be able to articulate the doctrine and dogma of the gospel but feel as though we're doing so from the outside looking in.

I want to better understand how we got here, the reasons we feel this resistance, and the ways we've intentionally and unintentionally cultivated it. Most of all, I want to try to describe how we might live differently.

Much of what's ahead is an extended conversation with writers, thinkers, and artists who have also tried to reckon with this strange world. People like Hannah Arendt, Charles Taylor, James K. A. Smith, Helen Macdonald, and David Foster Wallace have described this world (and how we got here) in ways that make sense of my own experience. Hearing them, I felt a little less crazy and a little less lonely. In a few places, this book is also a reckoning with my own story.

Each chapter explores how we've been shaped by this strange world and what options are available for another way of living and seeing. After each chapter is a Pathway section—an attempt to describe specific practices that reshape how we live and experience the world. My hope is to gain a clearer understanding of both the challenges and the opportunities we have for a transformed way of life. If you happen to be reading this with a friend or in a group, you might want to read both a chapter and a Pathway for each discussion.

Last, on any one of the topics ahead, I want to acknowledge that I'm just scratching the surface. What's ahead is almost like a walking tour of a city—a casual stroll where I'll point some things out and tell an interesting story or two along the way. My goal was not to be comprehensive (and not to be boring) but to provoke some different ways of seeing.

So, here it is. Like my cat on the front porch, I feel a little worse for the wear now that it's done, but most of all, I feel excited to share. I believe the world isn't quite what we've been led to think it is. Like Susanna Clarke's England, I think there's some magic yet to be discovered. Here's hoping I can convince you.

ONE

Discovering Our Disenchantment

I stumbled upon my disenchantment a few years ago after attending a dedication service at my parents' church. The new, eighty-million-dollar facility was roughly the size of the Death Star, with a parking lot that rivaled Six Flags in pure concrete acreage. There were more volunteers directing traffic and opening doors than most churches have for attendees.

During the service, a "special music" number was sung by an unironically mustachioed man in a suit, a contemporary Christian power ballad with swooning strings and multiple key changes. About midway through the song, a large cross on the back wall began to glow.

To be clear: when I say large, I mean *large*. The eight-thousand-seat auditorium has two balconies, and the distance from the stage to the catwalk above it is probably four stories. The cross spanned most of that height, a simple brown cross on a beige wall.

At first, the glow was subtle—a pale fluorescence around the edges that one might have dismissed as a weird reflection. But it soon became clear that there was some serious wattage behind it. As the mustachioed man stairstepped keys from the bridge to the final chorus, the light grew brighter and brighter—like, migraine-inducing bright—casting long, stark shadows on the stage.

The song ended and the crowd roared with applause, many wiping tears on their arms as they leapt to their feet and clapped. Eventually, the glow diminished and the house lights came up and the service moved along. All the lights retained a standard, this-worldly brightness for the remainder of the service.

At lunch afterward, between bites of chain-restaurant lasagna, my dad asked, "What did you think?"

"What do you mean?" I said.

"The cross . . . what did you think? It was pretty bright, right?"

I nodded.

"Do you think," he hesitated, and then said in a lower voice, "Do you think it was *real*?"

I pushed a forkful of overcooked noodles through a grey puddle of alfredo sauce that I regretted ordering. Then I searched his face. "What do you mean?" I repeated.

"The light," Dad said. "It was awfully bright."

"Do you mean, like, was it a miracle?" I asked.

Dad leaned back. "I mean, it probably wasn't," he said. He scooped up a slab of lasagna, grinned, and said, "Right?"

My dad's a civil engineer. When I was a kid, he designed airport runways. He could bore you senseless talking about the different load-bearing capacities of concrete, their response to heat and pressure, which one you'd want to pour in your basement and which is good for dropping a 747 out of the sky onto.

He's highly rational, and though he takes his faith seriously, he's not the type of person who would send cash to televangelists for prayer towels or get in line to be slain by the Spirit. I have seen him tear up once or twice in a church service, but to be fair, I'd guess he's also cried at more than one Pixar movie. He definitely got misty during the last episode of ALF. There's a big difference between being sentimental and superstitious, and yet, here he was, raising the possibility that the glow behind a cross in a multi-million-dollar facility with state-of-the-art audio, video, and lighting was some kind of miracle.

At the time, dad's question seemed so odd, so out of character. But this isn't my dad's story; it's mine. It's the story of how I stumbled upon my own disenchantment. Because what surprised me in retrospect was not that Dad raised the possibility of a miracle in a modern, industrial megachurch service; it was the utter impossibility of such a thing in my mind. Is it stranger to want to read a miracle into a stage effect, or to be a Christian whose gut-level reaction is "That's ridiculous"?

My guess is that most would react as I did: surprised and cynical. There are rational reasons for being cynical about this particular miracle, but it didn't take any thought or reasoning for me (or, in all likelihood, for you) to be skeptical. It was my instinct, my gut reaction. I didn't have to think first and stitch together my reasons for be-

> I am programmed to expect that the world is what I can see, touch, and measure.

lieving the light was ordinary. I *felt* that it was impossible for it to be supernatural and then found evidence to support my suspicions.

What I stumbled upon, then, was a deeply ingrained posture, a fully-formed attitude toward the world that is suspicious not only of well-timed miracles in the middle of a big production number, but is actually suspicious of any kind of religious experience.

I react to the suggestion of a miracle—or for that matter, any thoughts about God, the spiritual, or the transcendent—with skepticism and cynicism. It is my default setting.[1] I am programmed to expect that the world is what I can see, touch, and measure, and any thought or idea that runs against that expectation is met with resistance. Programming is actually a great way to think about it. I have learned to see the world this way, and I don't have to think about it anymore.

I don't think I'm alone. I believe that most people experience something similar—a subtle-but-strong resistance to faith and a skepticism toward anything that veers toward the supernatural.

This way of seeing the world is what Charles Taylor calls disenchantment.[2] A disenchanted world has been drained of magic, of any supernatural presences, of spirits and God and transcendence. A disenchanted world is a material world, where what you see is what you get.

It's not a world entirely without God or a world without religion. Rather, it's a world where God and religion are superfluous. You can believe whatever you want so long as you don't expect it to affect your everyday experience. Believe whatever you want about God or the afterlife, but trust in science and technology to explain everything about the real world.

We didn't choose to think and feel this way. It's simply the world of ideas we inhabit, a thousand stories told and repeated about how the world works. Christians and non-Christians alike are disenchanted because we're all immersed in a world that presents a material understanding of reality as the plausible and grown-up way of thinking. Even people from faith traditions more open to mystery or miraculous works of the Spirit will experience this to some degree or another. It's the way the Western world frames its ideas.

Perhaps to best understand disenchantment, we can look at its opposite, the "enchanted" world of a few centuries ago. In that world, men and women saw themselves as spiritual creatures, vulnerable to blessings and curses, to angels and demons, and subject to the god or gods who made and oversaw the world. This enchanted world was part of a Cosmos,[3] an orderly creation full of meaning, a place with a purposeful origin and a clear destination, guaranteed by the god or gods who made it and rule over it. At the same time, this Cosmos is full of mystery, a place where our knowledge has its limits and an unseen spiritual realm is constantly at work, shaping our everyday experience.

In disenchantment, we no longer live in a Cosmos; we live in a universe, a cold, hostile place whose existence is a big accident, where humanity is temporarily animated "stuff" that's ultimately meaningless and destined for the trash heap.

Bravery in this disenchanted world means facing the emptiness head-on. Comedian Louis CK described this on Conan O'Brien's late night talk show. Louis was talking about why he wouldn't let his kids have cell phones, which led him to talk about his own sense of emptiness:

What the phones are taking away is the ability to just sit there. That's being a person. Because underneath everything in your life there is that thing, that empty, forever empty. That knowledge that it's all for nothing and that you're alone. It's down there.

And sometimes when things clear away, you're not watching anything, you're in your car, and you start going, "Oh no, here it comes. That I'm alone." It starts to visit on you. Just this sadness. Life is tremendously sad, just by being in it. . . .

That's why we text and drive. I look around, pretty much 100 percent of the people driving are texting. And they're killing, everybody's murdering each other with their cars. But people are willing to risk taking a life and ruining their own because they don't want to be alone for a second because it's so hard.[4]

In a disenchanted world, solitude is terrifying. We are alone. The universe is "empty, forever empty." Louis and others like him argue that facing that emptiness is the right thing to do. Accept the cold, harsh reality of the real world.

Louis makes explicit a vision of the world that shapes us whether we know it or not. Our culture rehearses stories, ideas, and dialogues that shame us away from any kind of belief in transcendence. Charles Taylor calls these "disciplines of disenchantment." "We regularly . . . accuse each other of 'magical' thinking, of indulging in 'myth,' of giving way to 'fantasy'; we say that X isn't living in our century, that Y has 'mediaeval' mind, while Z, whom we admire, is way ahead of her time."[5]

These disciplines prime us to respond to the world much like Pavlov primed his dog to salivate at the sound of a ringing bell. When we are regularly shamed away from thoughts that venture near spirituality and transcendence, we learn to avoid it altogether, even in our thoughts. We develop a resistance to thoughts that would carry us outside of the world of the visible, measurable, or scientifically verifiable.

~

Philosopher and social theorist Hannah Arendt says this way of seeing the universe began with Galileo, who revealed that the

Earth (and humanity) wasn't the center of the universe.[6] His discovery called into question the story we'd been telling about who we were and what kind of world we lived in. If the earth wasn't at the center of the universe, did it still make sense to imagine all of history as a divine drama, unfolded by God for his glory and our good? Were we actually just one story of many, one planet of many, adrift in a meaningless cosmic sea?

At the same time, the universe revealed itself to be more vast, more hostile, and more empty than we'd previously imagined. It also revealed itself to be more knowable than we'd imagined, yielding its secrets as we developed the technology to unlock them—the telescope, the microscope, the atomic bomb, the Hadron collider. Technology has given us the sense that everything within the universe can be made to appear to our senses and harnessed for our purposes.[7] It may be meaningless, but it can be comprehended and mastered.

This mastery, though, is a bit of an illusion as well. The accumulated body of scientific knowledge can tell us all about the canvas, oils, and minerals that combine to make a work of art, but they cannot tell us why it takes our breath away.

Modern knowledge involves breaking things down into component parts. As philosopher Michel Foucault argues in *The Birth of the Clinic*, nowhere is this more disturbingly clear than in modern medicine, which came not out of the development of knowledge about the health and thriving of human bodies but out of the study of dead bodies, exhumed, dissected, and evaluated.

It is undeniable that this kind of knowledge has value. But Arendt's point—and many others have joined her—is to call into question whether this kind of knowledge is the only way of knowing something and, moreover, whether it's the best way of knowing something.

Dallas Willard once wrote that while you will not find him apart from his body, the surest way to never find him would be to tear his body open looking for him. There is a mysterious wholeness about a person. Whatever you might know about their bio-chemistry, anatomy, psychology, and biography cannot account for who they are and what being with them feels like. Likewise, the total knowledge of how fusion makes stars burn, how light travels through the solar system, and how the gases in our atmosphere refract and bend that light is less wonderful than beholding a sunset. A food chemist who can tell you all about what a strawberry is—how it grows, what its chemical makeup is, why the tongue tells the brain it's sweet—somehow knows less than a child who has actually tasted one. And wouldn't we all agree that the child's knowledge is superior? More useful? Or at the very least, more conducive to a good life?

The average grandma can't tell you much about amino acids and protein chains, but hours at the stove have taught her not to salt the tomato sauce until it's reduced. She can tell by the way a pork chop resists pressure from a spatula whether or not it's done, and she knows that the acidity of limes can cut the heat in a curry. Do you want her or the chemist making your dinner?

What we're talking about is the difference between knowing—a category we might use to describe abstracted knowledge like the kind that leads to success on tests and money on *Jeopardy!*—and know-how—a kind of knowing that's more integrated with life, or better put, more integrated with the body. It is a lived-in knowing and an experienced knowing.

The Bible is treated like any other object in a disenchanted world. Our common approach is to study it, and by *study* we mean something akin to the study of science or the study of language. The Bible is anatomized, broken into its component parts. To really understand it, we must understand first-century Judaism, the original languages, and the systematic theologies, which are the frame across which we can spread it.

This ends up polarizing the church's approach to the Bible. On the one hand, some feel no need to preserve the Bible as inerrant or infallible, and so the Bible is picked apart, what's true sorted from what's false according to the currents of cultural whim. This approach, taken by everyone from Thomas Jefferson to the Jesus Seminar to the current revisionism around sexuality, tells us that Scripture comes from an ignorant social context, which allows critics to separate socially acceptable Biblical ideas—humanism, pacifism, benevolence, and mercy—from those that are now unacceptable, such as belief in the supernatural or sexual ethics.

On the other hand, some try to squeeze the Bible through the lenses of disenchantment in another way. Here, the authority of the Bible is maintained, but the Bible must act like any other modern text—like a textbook or the instruction book that comes with a cordless drill. This demands a rigid literalism and leads to attitudes like *30 Rock*'s Kenneth Parcel, who said his favorite subject in school was science, where they studied the Old Testament. Kenneth is a good fundamentalist, and as James K. A. Smith puts it, "No one is more modern than a fundamentalist."[8]

The important thing to note is that the approach of liberals and fundamentalists is much the same. The text has no life of its own. It isn't a living whole—a breathing, fiery creature full of mystery, something to be approached with care and humility; it's a subject to be mastered, a corpse to be dissected. It's placed on a steel table and subjected to a thousand acts of violence. It is split into its component parts, footnoted for historicity, and commented on from every angle. In effect, it becomes hedged behind high walls of specialized knowledge, and most Christians—unless they've spent many hours in classes or in inductive Bible studies—are as frightened to talk about what a text might mean as they are to answer a question in a math or science class. Better to save it for the experts and leave it untouched.

If by chance they have applied themselves to many hours of study, they become (as Professor Snape once described Hermione Granger in *Harry Potter*) an "insufferable know-it-all." They have a frightening certainty. The text has been mastered, the questions all answered. Their Bible has no mysteries; it is all knowable now.

What remains after this treatment is an abstraction. For disenchanted Christians, the Bible is the source of knowledge about God, the gospel, and the spiritual life. Nothing is sacred but the Bible, but of course, by that we don't mean *this* Bible or *that* Bible. We don't mean any *actual* Bible in existence—because what was sacred and God-breathed was the Bible in its original manuscripts, and we don't possess any of those.

What remains is not the Word of God but the *idea* of the Bible: an abstract, theoretical Bible that is perfect and perfectly out-of-reach for any and all of us. As a result, we are necessarily thrown into a posture of suspicion about everything we encounter in the spiritual life—every text, every sermon, every person's testimony. We must ask, "Does it fit?" Does it fit into the schema we've adopted that frames our thinking about the Bible? Are we *certain* that we're right?

This way of knowing breeds fear in two ways. On the one hand, we fear attacks from the outside, from unbelievers, on the Bible's reliability. On the other, we're afraid of ourselves, worried that we might not know enough or worse, that we might believe the wrong idea. This fear causes us to double-down on our disenchanted approach to the Bible, coming back with a scalpel to dissect it again and to look for the evidence that supports the Bible's historicity and our beliefs about it. This is a quest for certainty.

To be sure, these things matter immensely. We need to know we can trust the Bible, and we need to feel confident that we believe the right things about it. But in many ways, I fear that many Christians are stuck there and that the Bible is never more than an object for analysis for them, as opposed to it being the voice of the Beloved. We can master it like the periodic table of elements or the statistics of the New York Yankees while keeping it divorced from real life.

If the Bible *is* the voice of the Beloved, then there must be a way of reading it that connects with us as whole people, just as knowing and being known in a relationship is a whole-person enterprise. There must be ways of reading and engaging Scripture that strike us at the level of our emotions, our imagination, and our bodies.

To return to the food and cooking metaphor, there's a way of talking about food that leaves us ignorant of its flavors. With Scripture, we need to find pathways that enable us to taste and see that the Lord is good, to borrow a phrase.

We hunger for that kind of know-how, for a relationship with Scripture that leads to something deeper than head knowledge. We long for wonder, and we long for communion with God, but we're so terrified of getting something wrong that we either avoid Scripture altogether or treat it as a cold, dead abstraction, unable to connect it to real life.

In *Hunting the Divine Fox*, Robert Farrar Capon—a writer and Episcopal priest—argued that this kind of dry, scholarly abstraction is a great way to miss the point of a text. Describing Genesis 1, he wrote:

> In the old days, when theologians were less uptight about their respectability in the eyes of biblical critics, the odd, majestic plural of that fateful "Let us make" [in Genesis 1:26] was always taken as one of the Old Testament evidences for the doctrine of the Trinity. Nowadays you lose your union card if you do things like that, but I still think it's nice. . . . What's nice about that "us" is precisely its oddness. It's the kind of mysteriously gratuitous detail that's so much fun to come across in the work of a master craftsman. . . .
>
> See? You need to play with Scripture or else you get it all wrong. Deriving the doctrine of the Trinity from the "us" is nothing more than a little bit of baroque ornamentation: it's legitimate as long as you keep things in balance. . . . You may not know exactly why it's there, but you feel it's trying to tell you something, trying to elicit some kind of response from you.

He invites us to an approach that is

> perfectly serious and perfectly silly at the same time. Which is just great. It's like making love; you can laugh while you do it. As a matter of fact, if you don't, at least sometimes, you're probably a terrible lover. Watch out for Biblical commentators, therefore, who sound as if they're holding a sex manual in the other hand.[9]

Lovemaking might be the perfect way to think about the problem with disenchanted readings of the Bible. Lovers might study technique, but they never mistake it for the "point" of lovemaking. They're after something deeper, something more akin to communion. They surrender to one another. They want to encounter the *person*, and the great gift that lovers can give to one another is their undivided attention and presence.

Failing that, we feel cold, distant, lonesome, and used.

If, on some level, we're doubtful of the presence of an actual God in our actual world, it's no wonder that we might confuse abstracted, technical knowledge of the Bible with a spiritual life. How often have you encountered someone whose knowledge of the Bible is encyclopedic but whose presence is harsh, dark, or miserable? How often do you hear clichéd stories about Christians with all the right answers that stiff waiters on tips, are horrible to their spouses or neighbors, and who you wouldn't trust with your dog?

The unchanged lives of Christians who have tremendous knowledge of the Bible highlight two of the great consequences of our disenchantment. We think knowledge of the Bible is all that matters, so we fail to attend to our character, our soul, and our relationships. Our way of living the Christian life leaves all of these things unchanged.

We need a way of thinking about the Scriptures that allows us to come to it as whole persons—who think, feel, and imagine—and find nourishment on all levels. We need to preserve the Bible's character as personal speech exchanged between the Lover and the Beloved. The voice that rings from the Bible is the voice of the one we long to hear from, long to know, long to find our rest in.

A while back, my wife and I spent an evening at a cabin in the woods celebrating a friend's birthday with several other couples. I woke early the next morning to go for a run on a trail that led through the woods to a pond on the other side of a rocky hill. It was a cold fall morning, and the path was covered in leaves and dense fog.

As I ran, I saw something on the ground that looked like pulled taffy, parallel ribbons and threads, curled, white, and translucent. I stopped to pick up a piece of it and was astonished at its lightness. I turned and looked back down the path and noticed more of it along the edges of the path and up the hillside into the woods, tangled in vines and leaves.

Looking back at the piece in my hand, it reminded me of the geometry of conch shells. It was beautiful. I picked up another piece and crushed it in my hand. It immediately became a fine powder.

I went back to the cabin and brought a few friends out to the woods to see them. We were all mystified. It felt like we were in the opening scene of a science fiction movie: aliens had landed in the night and left these ghostly shells as the only evidence of their presence.

But in the age of smartphones and Google, it didn't take long to get an explanation. They're called frost flowers, and they appear in the late fall and early winter. As the air temperature drops below freezing, plant stems contract, squeezing sap and water out into the air, forming ribbons of crystal. It's relatively rare, but perfectly explainable.

And yet, I don't believe this explanation is sufficient. While we might be able to trace the physics of frost flowers, does that account for their beauty or for the way they captivated us that morning? Is it better to describe them as one more meaningless thing in a meaningless universe, or as the gesture of an artist?

> Is it possible that the truth of the world isn't something we can test and measure?

There's a line in *Indiana Jones and the Last Crusade* where Indy tells a group of students, "Archeology is the search for fact, not truth. If it's truth you're looking for, Dr. Tyree's philosophy class is right down the hall." I wonder if we wouldn't benefit a little from this distinction, too. If we think of facts as those measurable, verifiable ways of seeing the world, and if we think of truth as the bigger narrative that makes sense of them and ties them together, then we might say that Western culture has been consumed with the quest for facts for the last few hundred years but has lost sight of the truth along the way. Is it possible that the truth of the world isn't something we can test and measure? Is it possible that there are layers of our experience that lie beyond our physical senses, layers that reveal themselves in the way our hearts ache when we see beautiful things, or in the powerful love and burdening we feel at the birth of a child, or even in the darkness we sense when sorrows strike?

Is it possible that we dwell in a Cosmos, not a universe, and that a moment like this one—when beauty stops us in our tracks—is an encounter with something more than frozen water and sap, something more like a love letter?

Maybe the facts of frost flowers don't tell us the truth of frost flowers.

Our faith is uniquely challenged today, but it's false to think that a challenged faith is unique. The Scriptures tell a story of counter-cultural faith, and they always have. Where we are challenged by a disenchanted milieu, previous generations sought God down the street from temples to sex goddesses and across the river from the Pantheon, or had to uncover the gospel in an era of Christendom when the church's political power obscured its spiritual power. In all times and places, the good news has been challenged by counter-feits and competitors.

In our age, we need to know whether there's someone on the other end of the line when we pray. We need to know whether that person is a superfluous, disinterested deity or a loving Father whose eye is on the sparrow, who is acquainted with suffering and grief, who rejoices over us with singing. And while not all Christians have lived with our particularly modern doubts, many of them are as old as humanity. *What kind of God is this? How can I know him? Can he answer the questions about life and meaning that simmer just under the surface of my thoughts?*

Our world offers answers to these questions. Louis CK's comments are one example: be brave, face the void of meaninglessness. That approach hums in the background of our lives and whether we like it or not, shapes our experience of faith.

In contrast, the prophet Jeremiah calls us to consider an "ancient path." When he spoke those words, Israel had abandoned their God, and Jeremiah was inviting them to come home:

> Thus says the Lord:
> "Stand by the roads, and look,
>   and ask for the ancient paths,
> where the good way is; and walk in it,
>   and find rest for your souls." (Jer 6:16)

The prophet invites us to consider a path that is profoundly counter-cultural. We live in an age obsessed with the new: new gadgets, new experiences, new sexual horizons—the list goes on and on. We think, *The last iPhone didn't satisfy my aching heart, but maybe this one will.* And that logic gets applied equally to consumer goods, jobs, and marriages.

Yet the prophet calls us to an ancient path. No need for innovation—to move forward we must look backward. To find the path we must "stand by the roads, and look." It's a call to stillness—to *stand* rather than to continue our aimless wandering, to resist the momentum of our chaotic world and look, think, consider where we're going and why. Hannah Arendt once wrote that we need to "think what we are doing," saying that the problem of our modern age is thoughtlessness. We live busy lives, and our thoughtlessness allows us to continue to be carried along in the currents of an unreflective culture. Arendt's thoughts echo Jeremiah's—stop, look, think, *pay attention.*

To embrace this invitation requires two things. First, we must understand that we already have a way of life. It's not enough to say the world is disenchanted; we must also acknowledge that *we* are disenchanted, and that we did it to ourselves. We have embraced ways of living—habits, practices, and stories that we're often unaware of—that prime us for disbelief and doubt. Our way of life presupposes that God is superfluous, and when we try to live as if he weren't, we discover a deep internal dissonance. Understanding what those habits and practices are and how they work on us is the first step.

The second step is embracing a different story and, with it, a different set of habits and practices. Here, we can begin to talk about what the church has historically called spiritual disciplines. But here we encounter difficulty again. At their best, the disciplines (such as prayer, Scripture reading, and fasting) are a way of life, habits that allow us to in-habit a reality. But that's not how the disciplines are usually discussed. Instead, there's an awful lot of finger-wagging, "have-you-read-your-Bible-today" spirituality, where the disciplines are part of a moral checklist that keeps God from being angry with us.

To see the disciplines in this way is not only to confuse their purpose, it's to confuse the gospel itself, which begins with the well-established fact that God is no longer angry with us. If we fail to understand the gospel, then the disciplines become a means to an end—a way of trying to earn God's attention and favor. But if our starting place with God is the radical grace extended through Jesus, then the spiritual disciplines are invitations, not obligations—ways of being with God, not appeasing him.

Jeremiah's words help us here too. We're not called first to act but to cease. Stand and look: the work that so much of our lives are spent frantically trying to accomplish—self-justifying spiritual work, a hunger to earn the approval of others, our own internal moralistic standards—has already been finished. Stop struggling to earn approval. All is accomplished in Jesus.

> If we fail to understand the gospel, then the disciplines become a means to an end—a way of trying to earn God's attention and favor.

Once we accept that finished work, we'll find an ancient path that allows us to walk more and more deeply into the remade world of God's kingdom. As we take up ancient practices like prayer, Scripture reading, and fasting, we will see the way they confront our disenchanted way of knowing the world. The kingdom is an enchanted place, and by God's grace, we can experience the kingdom's mystery and wonder throughout our lives.

In her gorgeous memoir, *H Is for Hawk*, Helen Macdonald tells the story of raising a goshawk after the death of her father. It's a story of grief, loss, and—in a way—resurrection as she works to teach this feral and powerful creature to fly and hunt with her. On one of her early (and failed) attempts to fly the hawk, she joins her friend Stuart in the English countryside. Disappointed that the hawk won't fly, they walk back through a field toward their cars:

Stuart stops dead.

"Stuart?"

"Look!" he says. "Look at that!"

"What?" I say, turning and shading my eyes. "I can't see anything."

"Look toward the sun."

"I am!"

"Look *down*!"

Then I see it. The bare field we'd flown the hawk upon is covered in gossamer, millions of shining threads combed downwind across every inch of soil. Lit by the sinking sun the quivering silk runs like light on water all the way to my feet. It is a thing of unearthly beauty, the work of a million tiny spiders searching for new homes. Each had spun a charged silken thread out into the air to pull it from its hatch-place, ascending like an intrepid hot-air balloonist to drift and disperse and fall. I stare at the field for a long time.[10]

What Macdonald experiences in that moment is revelation. Those shimmering threads had been there the whole time. While standing in the field, watching the hawk, willing it to fly, her world was cold and hostile. But given a few words, and standing in a different place, her way of seeing was transformed.

Our lives are very much about seeing. We talk about seeing opportunities or seeing a way forward. We train ourselves to see in certain ways, too, to see potential in an empty canvas or a blank page or in the raw ingredients of a meal. Athletes train to see the trajectory of a fastball or an opening in pass coverage. Once you've learned to see the world in certain ways, you don't have to think about it any more. It becomes automatic.

Jeremiah's invitation—and Jesus' invitation, too—is to see the world in a different way. "Stand by the roads, and look." It's an invitation that offers rest for our souls and reveals the world to be much more wondrous than we'd thought or feared. It's a world permeated by God's grace and filled with his presence, from the brightest to the darkest places—a world where everything is being reconciled and made new in Jesus.

What kind of world do we live in? Does it make the most sense to say that our encounters with beauty and wonder are happy accidents, random stimuli that happen to trigger our brain's pleasure center? Or is it possible that we live in a world where spider silks lit by the setting sun or a hillside flecked with frost flowers can be seen as something more than random?

We've feared it to be otherwise, and many have talked themselves into believing those fears are true, contented themselves with an empty universe. Low expectations protect us from disappointment. But Jeremiah's invitation—and Jesus' own—is to hope that the world is a place of meaning and love. Walking that ancient path, where the good way is, opens our eyes to see—and reside in—a different world.

PATHWAY 1
RE-ENCHANTING OUR WORLD

I've spent some time discussing what it means to be shaped by a disenchanted world. Key to that formation are disciplines of disenchantment. These aren't just ideas; they're often stories, and stories have a way of working on us at a deep level. For instance, it's one thing to hear someone say, "Life is random and meaningless." It's another to watch a movie like *Garden State* or *Castaway*. Movies capture the imagination, and these two in particular tell stories that erode a sense of meaning, order, and purpose in the world. Bravery, in each, is facing the randomness and meaninglessness of life.

This kind of storytelling is happening all the time in movies, novels, and music, but it's also happening in a kind of shorthand in everyday conversations, especially when they veer near the spiritual or supernatural. Not long ago, after a string of violent mass shootings, there was a social media uproar over the "thoughts and prayers" sentiment that often gets repeated after a tragedy. "Enough with your 'thoughts and prayers,'" people wrote. "*Do* something." While there's some degree of politicking going on in many of those tweets, there's also a bit of revelation about the way people see the world: thoughts and prayers are wasted in an empty universe. It's a perfect example of a world primed for disbelief.

So how do we change? How do we experience things differently?

We need to reorient our lives around a different set of stories. The people of God have always been storytellers. Starting with the exodus, God's people have been telling and retelling the story of their Savior. Even the Ten Commandments begin with a nod toward the story: "I am the LORD your God, *who brought you out of*

Egypt." God reminds Israel of their salvation before he calls them to a way of life.

Throughout the Old Testament, Israel's status as either righteous or rebellious roughly coincides with their faithfulness to remember (and tell) their story. Periodically, the story gets lost, the gods of neighboring tribes begin to appear in Israel's worship, and the nation falters. But then, someone finds the law, they read it, and a renewal movement begins.

Our situation today is much like theirs. We're called to worship competing "gods" who go by names like sex, money, power, and status, and like Israel, we need to remember the story of the God who rescued us from slavery to these lesser gods.

In the New Testament, storytelling continues. Every sermon in the book of Acts is a retelling of the story of God's salvation through Jesus. The sacraments that lie at the heart of Christian worship— baptism and communion—are shorthand symbols for the story of Jesus' death, resurrection, and the restoration of all things.

If we want to leave behind our disenchantment, we have to find ways to immerse ourselves in these stories. We have to counter the stories of our disenchanted world.

To do this, I want to suggest that we think in terms of marking time. By marking time, I mean that our lives should have signposts and landmarks, significant moments that call us to remember that we are citizens of a different world.

I like thinking about this in terms of concentric circles. Each circle narrows to a shorter interval of time: yearly, weekly, daily, hourly.

MARKING TIME

Yearly. In a given year, most Christians have at least two significant moments that call them back to God: Christmas and Easter. These two holidays are anchor points in our calendar. Christmas is ordinarily preceded by a time of anticipation called Advent—remembering the longing of Israel and the longing of the world for a savior. Christmas, with its feasts, its practice of gift-giving, and all the lights and tinsel that come along with it, is meant to be an over-the-top celebration of the generosity and mercy of God.

Likewise, Easter is normally preceded by a season of anticipation called Lent. In Lent, the church historically takes a long fast and spends forty days preparing for Easter with a time of repentance and lament. Good Friday is the deepest day of mourning, and on Easter, everything changes. The church is decorated with flowers, a feast is laid out on the table, and everyone gathers to shout, "He is risen! He is risen indeed."

Here, too, our families typically gather and celebrate. Easter and the days around it can be a particularly dynamic feast—remembering Holy Thursday and the Passover, fasting for Good Friday, and feasting again to celebrate the resurrection.

Whatever your church tradition is, there's value in marking out these days as sacred (or if you don't like that term, then call them "unique"). By celebrating them, you mark your own life with the two most significant moments in the life of Jesus. Not only that, you stand with Christians all over the world and all through the centuries who shaped their days with the story of God.

Weekly. Perhaps the most significant rhythm in our lives is gathering regularly with the church. It's significant because it's the most outward, Godward hour in our weeks, and because it's a time when the invisible is made visible: the scattered church comes together; the signs of the kingdom are present in bread and wine and in the waters of baptism. The gathered church is a foretaste of the new heaven and the new earth.

It often doesn't feel like a heavenly experience, though, and showing up can be difficult. As someone with young children, I'm as aware of this as anyone. It can be brutal getting your family organized and out the door. Once you're at church, it can be distracting to sit next to the crazy person who talks to themselves through the sermon. It can be frustrating when your church tries on a new musical or stylistic identity, and you have a hard time participating. And yet, again and again, the Scriptures tell us that gathering with the church is necessary (Heb 10:25) and that Christ dwells with his people in a unique and rich way when we gather and sing together (Col 3:16).

For these reasons and more, the gathering of the local church is like the heartbeat of the Christian life. It's a time when we unite with other believers and where we can look around and remember "I am not alone." In a disenchanted world, that's more important than ever.

Weekly habits might also include regular practices like fasting or feasting, or gatherings like small groups, accountability groups, family dinners, and more. Each of these is a way of marking our time and calling our attention back to the kingdom of God.

Daily. Daily disciplines include journaling, praying, reading Scripture, and many more. For now, the specifics aren't important. (I'll explore many of them in the pages ahead and explore thinking through daily routines after chapter seven.) What's important is to begin thinking in terms of daily habits. How are we marking our time on a day-to-day basis so that we're regularly rooting ourselves in this bigger story?

Hourly. The final circle is moment-by-moment. How do we go about our days in a way that sustains an awareness that we live in another world? Paul talks about "praying unceasingly." Brother Lawrence wrote about "practicing the presence of God"—an effort to fill his mind constantly with the knowledge of God's presence. Frank Laubach, a missionary, wrote about a "game with minutes" in which he trained himself to turn his thoughts to God minute-by-minute throughout the day.

While these might be lofty goals, I want to start much more simply, with a practice known as breath prayers.

BREATH PRAYERS

Breath prayers are exactly what they sound like: prayers that can be said in a single breath. To practice this discipline—which has been shared by Christians for many ages—you simply take in a deep, calming breath and, while exhaling, pray quietly or aloud a simple phrase meant to reorient you to God's presence, his kingdom, and his good will for you. It's a practice that brings the whole person—heart, mind, and body—back to an awareness of God's presence.

Many people begin this practice with the Jesus Prayer: "Lord Jesus, have mercy on me." You might take a favorite verse of Scripture and adapt it. Matthew 11:28 can become "Lord, I am weary, give me rest." Romans 8:1 can be prayed as a reminder that "there is no condemnation." For me, Colossians 3:3 has merged with a line from Augustus Toplady's hymn, "Rock of Ages": "Let me hide myself in thee." Each phrase is like the tip of an iceberg; it reaches back into a deeper, richer story and roots us in a larger, God-filled world.

The beauty of this practice is in its portability. There is no place, no meeting, no encounter in life where one can't stop and take a slow, deep breath. If you practice it regularly, you'll find yourself whispering prayers without having to think too much about it; they'll simply be part of life.

I believe these concentric circles can frame out our lives, filling them with touchstones that call us back to God's kingdom. They are a practical way of re-enchanting our world and our experiences, signposts on our journey that remind us that the world is far bigger, far more wondrous, and far more mysterious than we have been told.

TAKING STEPS

Take an inventory of your practices in each of the circles. Write them out: yearly, weekly, daily, hourly. For each category, ask yourself three questions:

- How consistent are these practices?
- How helpful are these practices?
- What's a step I could take in this circle to deepen and enrich these practices?

Habits and practices are only sustainable when they're valued in our communities and families, so be sure to talk with your family and closest friends about all of this. Consider how you might take steps to value these things more deeply together.

TWO

Modern Religious Sacrifices and the God Who Ends Religion

I witnessed a ritual sacrifice in the middle of a cool, third-wave coffee shop the other day. It's the sort of place that attracts herds of bearded hipsters and where they brew your coffee by hand, one cup at a time. I was sitting at a long row of benches against the wall, watching the crowd as they ordered, mingled, and eventually collected their meticulously crafted drinks from a stern-faced barista wearing an ironic t-shirt and a fedora.

A guy in his twenties, wearing skinny jeans, a plaid shirt, and a beanie (which might as well have been the clientele's uniform) came in carrying a heavy book. It looked like a nice academic volume—hardcover, black cloth binding, nice paper. He ordered and sat at a table near the middle of the shop, scanning his phone while waiting for his drink to come up at the bar. After collecting it, he returned to the table near the center of the room and began his rather embarrassing and earnest religious display.

He was arranging his book and his latte so that he could take a picture of them with his phone. He spent five minutes doing this, and I assure you that although five minutes might seem like a very long time to spend doing something like this, I'm certain that it was five minutes because I clocked him (which says something about me, I know). He tried capturing the image with the book on its side, next to the latte. Then he tried a few with the spine open to hold the book upright, the latte in front of it.

He wasn't finished. He then attempted several shots with the coffee cup perched on top of the book, but—I'm guessing here—the light wasn't good enough to capture both the latte art and the title of the book. Eventually, he started taking images with the book in his hand, including a few attempts without the latte at all. I began to worry about his latte growing cold and the foam turning dry and ugly. Eventually, he captured an image with the book on its side, propped up by his hand at an angle behind the cup. He tapped the phone's screen for a while, editing and posting the photo online. Finally, he set his phone down and began to drink his latte. Then he opened the book.

Now here's the best part. I swear he looked at the book for at most forty-five seconds. He flipped it open, thumbed a page or two, his eyes blank and disinterested, and then closed it and pulled out his phone again to see what kind of response the image got.

A moment or two later, my wife texted me. I alerted her about the keen observations I was making in the coffee shop. She told me to get back to writing. Then she asked which shop I was in. I told her, and moments later, she texted me the image the guy had posted to Instagram, which blew my mind. "You're like Batman," I said. She took this for the high praise it was.

Only when I saw the image, though, did I notice the title of the book. It was John Frame's *The Doctrine of the Word of God*. Perhaps it would have been slightly more ironic if the book had been Neil Postman's *Amusing Ourselves to Death*, or Jacques Ellul's *The Humiliation of the Word*, but this one was nearly perfect: a book about the primacy of God's Word as a prop in a social media post.

Religion is the business of appeasing gods. In the old days, you'd take some unfortunate animal to a temple, give it to a priest, and the priest would dispatch of it for you before the watchful eyes of whatever god, goddess, or demigod was in attendance. Hopefully, if the animal was in good enough condition, or if the god, goddess, or demigod was in a good enough mood, the priest would return with a blessing, sending you on your way with the knowledge that you'd satisfied him/her/it. If you were a true believer, the whole thing was done with a lot of love, care, and attention. And although most of us don't attend temples or make flesh-and-blood sacrifices, the religious impulses that drive all that activity are deeply human and inescapable.

These days, our sacrifices are virtual. We take an image. We type up a few thoughts. We edit and crop and shape them until they're just right—the finest specimen we can offer—and we extend them, via digital mediators, to a pantheon of little gods that wait to judge our work. If we gain their favor, they award us with likes, favorites, comments, and repostings. If not, the results can be the pain of echoing silence—or worse, we might incur their wrath.

It's not uncommon to read articles about how technology has made all of us narcissists. To an extent, I'm sympathetic to that view; it certainly seems to operate as though the whole world was meant to cater to our preferences. But I think the problem runs much deeper, and the real trouble began long before the invention of smartphones and social media.

I have cringe-inducing memories of my relationship with a mirror we had in the house growing up. It was a full-length mirror that sat in the hallway outside my childhood bedroom. It had a big brass-colored frame and a little table with matching brass-colored legs and a marble top that sat about mid-shin height underneath it. If you bumped your leg on the table en route to the bathroom in the middle of the night, it was murder.

But I have much more cringe-worthy memories of standing in front of the thing before school would start each year. No matter whether it was the fourth grade or the tenth, the look on my face was essentially the same. I was asking a question: Is this me?

In the fourth grade, I asked it while wearing Zubaks and a Hulk Hogan t-shirt. I asked it in the seventh grade while wearing acid-washed jeans and a silk button-up shirt. Just a year or two later, I asked it while wearing a tattered cardigan from the Salvation Army and a Smashing Pumpkins t-shirt. In high school, I went through a phase that involved Abercrombie & Fitch sweaters that I hoped would impress a girl (they did not). The question remained the same: Is this me?

I was always trying to prepare a new version of myself to present to the people around me, a version that improved on the one I lived with. I even tried to change the way I walked. Cool kids stood tall. They walked with confidence and swagger—two qualities I seem, eternally, to lack. I'd walk toward the mirror, trying to look like anyone but myself. Usually this ended with me standing nose-to-nose with my unchanged image, exasperated sighs fogging the glass.

I used to think I was the only one who felt this way, but as I've grown older, I've come to believe that whatever this impulse is, there's something universal about it. The need to be seen in a certain way, to present a better, more put-together version of ourselves, shows up in the anxious Instagram posts of teenagers and the Twitter rants of Kanye West. It's present in the anxiety we feel around reunions and surprise encounters with old friends, and sometimes, it's present when the thought of going to work fills us with dread. Something deep within us is unsettled, and we want to appear to the world as better, more dignified, or more desirable—someone more beautiful or clever than the mope we see in the mirror.

In 1996, long before Skype or Facetime, David Foster Wallace predicted the rise and fall of videophones as part of a lengthy aside in his novel *Infinite Jest*. In Wallace's view, videophones weren't destined to last long because of the way they stirred up anxieties about how we're seen.

> Telephone calls could be fielded without makeup, toupee, surgical prostheses, etc. Even without clothes, if that sort of thing rattled your saber. But for the image-conscious, there was of course no such answer-as-you-are informality about visual-video telephone calls, which consumers began to see were less like having the good old phone ring than having the doorbell ring and having to throw on clothes and attach prostheses and do hair-checks in the foyer mirror before answering the door.[1]

To deal with this anxiety, people began wearing high-definition masks. One could quickly slip these on when the videophone rang in order to present a put-together, raptly attentive version of yourself to your caller. Soon, people began wearing masks to be "undeniably better-looking on videophones than their real faces were in person."[2]

After this, masks were supplanted with "Transmittable Tableaus," which were "essentially a heavily doctored still-photograph, one of an incredibly fit and attractive and well-turned-out human being, someone who actually resembled the caller only in such limited respects as like race and limb-number."

While masks and tableaus have yet to hit the market for users of Facetime and Skype, Wallace's vision of the future seems not far from the truth. Social media has led to an enormous amount of anxiety. Doctored photos are the norm not only in mass media but in the stuff ordinary folks post online every day. Apps like Facetune and Pixtr will make your face more symmetrical, your skin smoother, and your teeth whiter. Apps like SkinneePix and SkinnyCam make you appear ten pounds lighter. And if digital enhancement isn't enough, there's the "Facetime Facelift," a plastic surgery procedure that is designed to make sure you look better while pointing your phone's camera at your face.[3]

An incredible amount of energy goes into curating our online personas. Kim Kardashian, the patron-saint of social media, once said she "needed" about 1,200 selfies per day in order to get the good ones that she could post online. She's an extreme example, to be sure, but she shines light on the promise of social media: the chance to carefully edit and display the best version of ourselves to the world. The result is that people increasingly prefer online interaction to face-to-face. We can display a version of ourselves that, if not better looking, may be more witty, smart, generous, or compassionate.

And, of course, long before Twitter, Facebook, and Instagram, human beings found innumerable ways to present and preen and pretend we had ourselves put together. We've been spending billions of dollars on makeup, weight-loss programs, self-help programs, and pseudo-religious means of discovering our "best life now" for a long time. Social media merely streamlined the feedback loop for these efforts, making relationships more transactional and less intimate than ever before.

We are anxious people, covering our flaws, shaping our image, straining to present an acceptable version of ourselves to the world around us. And of course, all of this is merely symptomatic of a deeper issue. We don't just want to appear pretty or skinny or smart—we want to be good, acceptable, lovable. We want to know that we're approved. But in a world drained of transcendence, there is only the approval of the mob to fill the void.

Charles Taylor describes all this approval-seeking as "mutual display."[4] In mutual display, my life and the cultural world I occupy are always meant to be seen. I am projecting a version of myself in search of affirmation—maybe not from everyone but certainly those who I esteem. If I want to know that I'm okay, I need to hear it not from God or history but from the voices around me. And so life is lived with a constant eye on the surrounding mob in search of their affirmation and in search of confirmation that we're okay, that we belong. As James K. A. Smith puts it, this is why everyone these days acts like thirteen-year-old girls.[5]

The need for affirmation is spiritual, and the behavior it inspires is religious. The longing for acceptance is at the core of human experience and it shadows all of human history.

Behind this need for affirmation is the sense that something is wrong with us and, more deeply, that something is wrong with the world. In trying to make sense of our own brokenness, we get religious— whether we're offering goats to a lizard-god or selfies to Instagram followers. Likewise, our self-improvement efforts

> The need for affirmation is spiritual, and the behavior it inspires is religious.

are often aimed at the need for affirmation. Yes, some people genuinely do Crossfit, SoulCycle, and Weight Watchers because they want to feel healthier, and surely most who practice these things actually do feel better. But how much of this activity is also religious? How much is done in search of approval? Or redemption?

These are religious impulses, and they fit inside bigger religious stories that attempt to explain what's wrong with us and what's wrong with the world. The Greeks had the Pantheon, Prometheus, and Pandora's Box. Buddhists have a cyclical explanation of history and time. Hindus believe that the universe comes from Shiva, Brahma, and Vishnu. In each case, these religions offer some sense of explanation for our origins, our present situation, and our ultimate destination. These stories are meaning making, sense making, and ordering of our world.

In a disenchanted world, we have our own overarching narrative, and its cornerstone is progress—a sense that the world is moving from disorder to order, that humanity is improving not just biologically and evolutionarily but morally, intellectually, and spiritually.

This story accounts for why religion is so easily dismissed. We have evolved. We know better now. Religious people are clinging to a past that humanity should have moved beyond.

Likewise, the religious story of progress leads to religious attitudes about health and fitness. The only universally recognized sins in the high halls of progress are smoking and consuming corn syrup. As with religion, we know better. Evolve already.

What all religions share in common—from Athenian worshipers, to cults that eat the dead, to SoulCycle disciples—is a sense that the world is neatly divided into those who are in and those who are out. The in-group has found enlightenment, adheres to the right moral code, and makes the right blood-and-sweat sacrifices.

There's a Christian version of this religious storytelling too. In that story, Adam and Eve were rule keepers right up until the moment they ate from the forbidden fruit, and from that moment forward, they were rule breakers. That simple division is a way to frame all of Biblical history.

The law, given to Moses, told rule breakers how to be rule keepers, but all of Israel's efforts to live that life for any sustained period of time fell short. So God sent Jesus—the ultimate rule keeper—to die for rule breakers and forgive them. This gospel is fundamentally about liberation from the burden of the rules and liberation from the burden of being a rule breaker.

In this version of the story, religion—the effort of reconciling God and man (or, reconciling man with the universe, or man with himself)—is born in the aftermath of the fall. We have to reckon with our brokenness, and religion gets invented in an effort to make things right. In this version of the story, Jesus is the ultimate religious person, accomplishing what all of our efforts failed to do. Christianity as a whole can criticize all the other religions of the world because it's the only one that gets religion right.

This reading of Genesis 3 is the version of the story that's most familiar to me after a lifetime in the church and a childhood spent in Sunday school and Bible studies. The trouble is not only that it's reductionistic but also that it may be misleading in a way that perpetuates the trouble that Adam and Eve started in in the first place.

In *God Against Religion*, Matthew Myer Boulton retraces the events of Genesis 3 and describes a version of the fall of humanity that goes far beyond the familiar bedtime story about trees and fruit. As Boulton sees it, Genesis 3 isn't fundamentally a story about broken *rules* but broken *communion*, and the trouble begins before anybody eats anything.

The serpent arrives in the garden and asks Eve, "Did God actually say, 'You shall not eat of any tree in the garden'?" (Gen 3:1). Boulton writes, "The serpent effectively invites the man and woman to take up God's defense. 'Is God a miser?' he asks implicitly. 'Has God prohibited the very food you need to live?' In short, 'Has God denied you life?'"[6] Boulton likens this to the opening question of a catechism—a question like "What is the chief end of man?" In this case, the serpent isn't asking an honest question and isn't seeking an honest answer. He wants, instead, to awaken humanity's desire to "do well"—to "demonstrate their own excellent grasp of God's intentions."[7] He wants to inspire them to perform their righteousness. He wants to make them religious.

Eve responds by saying, "We may eat of the fruit of the trees in the garden" (Gen 3:2), but as Boulton points out, she doesn't stop there. "Like so many of her progeny, she preaches for too long! . . . As if to certify and make a show of their own impeccable orthodoxy and obedience, humans overstate the divine prohibition."[8] Eve continues, "But God said, 'You shall not eat of the fruit of the tree that is in the midst of the garden, neither shall you touch it, lest you die'" (Gen 3:3).

It wasn't enough for Eve to simply say, "We're not to eat of this one tree." She adds a command about touching it. In doing so

human beings confidently declare (a little too loudly) that they are beyond reproach, that they have been unimpeachably careful (indeed, more careful than God has instructed them to be), and thus that they do stand aright before God. With this apparently confident declaration, then, they betray their anxiety, deny their vulnerabilities, and thus deny their creatureliness. The hairline fissures grow wider. Now religion insinuates itself into the story. Because of this, Karl Barth called Eve the "first 'religious personality.'"[9]

Understood this way, sin can be seen as both a break from union with God and a break in trust with God. Before Genesis 3, Adam and Eve were perfect because they lived in perfect. What he prescribed for righteousness—*don't eat from that tree*—they trusted, believed, and obeyed. But when the serpent shows up, they make an attempt to take their righteousness a step further—*we don't even touch it*—and present themselves as "unimpeachably careful." It's a goodness that is independent of God, that doesn't need him, and it's a break from union with him.

What the serpent tempts them with—becoming "like God"—expands the cracks even further. Before this moment, the only life Adam and Eve knew was life-with-God. Now, conceptually, the possibility of life-against-God or life-apart-from-God appears, and God is conceived as someone separate and distant from humanity as opposed to someone in whom we "live and move and have our being." The serpent offers the possibility of self-improvement. *You can be like God if you eat from this tree.* He doesn't appeal to their sense of risk or forbidden pleasure. He appeals to them with religion: *Eat this meal with me and transcend your limitations. Live your best life now.*

Immediately afterward, their eyes are opened and they discover themselves naked and ashamed. Life-apart-from-God has begun, and their religious impulses are fully awakened. Their nakedness isn't new, only their shame and the need to improve upon their nakedness. So they rush to once again demonstrate their worth and independence. They knit fig leaves together to cover themselves, and they hide. In hiding, they reveal that their religious transformation is complete. They now believe themselves to be living in a world where they *can* hide from the watchful eye of God. It's an inversion of life before. Life-with-God is frightful and difficult to imagine. Life without him is not only possible but appealing.

This is the origin story for all our anxieties and our restless lives. Made for life-with-God, we were lured into life-apart-from-God, tempted by a religious impulse for self-improvement. Yielding to that temptation didn't result in transcendence; it exposed our flaws and weaknesses. We now know we're naked, and one religious effort—eating the fruit—leads to another—making fig-leaf clothing. And so it goes, throughout history. From the tower of Babel to Trump Tower, from Asheroth poles to selfie-sticks, from the golden calf to the Golden Globes, human history is one clawing effort after another toward self-improvement, self-advancement, and self-redemption.

In a way, this biblical narrative parallels the disenchantment narrative nicely. But where one sees progress, the other sees only false hope and disappointment.

Viewed this way, we can also see that Christianity offers the most harsh and damning criticism of religion in the history of the world. Religion isn't the solution to the problem of sin and evil; it's the source of it. All of our misguided efforts in our life-apart-from-God only exacerbate our loneliness, homelessness, and sorrow.

Perhaps no one said it better than Augustine: "Thou hast formed us for Thyself, and our hearts are restless till they find rest in Thee." We long for God. We long for home, for a life lived, breathed, and moved within him. Religion was birthed as a substitute for that life, an independent pathway to transcendence. But it fails, and it always failed.

This is why Robert Capon can say,

For Christians ... the entire religion shop has been closed, boarded up, and forgotten. The church is not in the religion business. It never has been and it never will be, in spite of all the ecclesiastical turkeys through two thousand years who have acted as if religion was their stock in trade. The church, instead, is in the Gospel-proclaiming business. It is not here to bring the world the bad news that God will think kindly about us only after we have gone through certain creedal, liturgical and ethical wickets; it is here to bring the world the Good News that "while we were yet sinners, Christ died for the ungodly." It is here, in short, for no religious purpose at all, only to announce the Gospel of free grace.[10]

Don't miss the point, as it relates to all we're talking about. Religion isn't just the "spiritual" stuff; it's everything we do to try and improve and present an approved version of ourselves to the world. Our disenchanted efforts at self-improvement and self-justification fail just as miserably as blood sacrifices and penitential lashings at reckoning with our brokenness. They might get you applause from the mob, and they might deliver a quick endorphin burst, but they cannot bring you home to God. They can't give you what you most long for.

> We don't need self-improvement; we need to come home.

Likewise, any approach to the Christian life that seeks self-improvement as the end goal will fail too. A life of prayer, fasting, and spiritual disciplines can easily be a life of empty religious effort if the goal isn't communion with God. We don't need self-improvement; we need to come home.

In his conflicts with the Pharisees, Jesus was pointed about the failure of religious effort.

> Woe to you, scribes and Pharisees, hypocrites! For you are like
> whitewashed tombs, which outwardly appear beautiful, but
> within are full of dead people's bones and all uncleanness. So
> you also outwardly appear righteous to others, but within you
> are full of hypocrisy and lawlessness. (Mt 23:27-28)

The version of ourselves that we project into the world is in-
adequate to reckon with our nakedness and exposure. We need
something more radical and more complete.

Elsewhere in Matthew, Jesus directly addresses the trouble of
living a life to please a mob. The mob didn't like John the Baptist
because he was somber and austere. They didn't like Jesus because
he kept with bad company and appeared to like food and drink too
much. They were like

> children sitting in the marketplaces and calling to their
> playmates,
>
> "We played the flute for you, and you did not dance;
> we sang a dirge, and you did not mourn." (Mt 11:16-17)

I imagine a crowd of gangly, menacing teenagers, leaning against
walls and doorways in an open air market. They have angry eyes
and sneering voices. They call out to individuals in the crowd,
mocking and shouting. They occasionally erupt in violence, sometimes amongst their own ranks, and sometimes in an effort to
snatch a bag or humiliate an unfortunate passerby.

You can't satisfy kids like these. Your attempts to do so will only
increase their demands. In spite of all of the signs and wonders that
accompanied Jesus' ministry, the mob sneered and mocked, demanding more, demanding that Jesus perform for them. He goes
on to condemn them, saying that even some of the Old Testament's

most cursed cities would have it easier on judgment day than those who sat in mocking judgment of Jesus.

Then he makes one of the most oft-quoted statements in all of the Gospels: "Come to me, all who labor and are heavy laden, and I will give you rest. Take my yoke upon you, and learn from me, for I am gentle and lowly in heart, and you will find rest for your souls. For my yoke is easy, and my burden is light" (Mt 11:28-30). The context is no coincidence. Jesus invites us to come to him as an alternative to trying to please the insatiable voices of the mob. The alternative to the disenchanted religion of display—a life spent seeking affirmation in the mirror of the world—is to find rest in Jesus.

Several years ago on Good Friday I went hiking on some trails near the Abbey of Gethsemani, a Cistercian monastery in the hills of Kentucky. I walked a long gravel road toward the woods and past a dilapidated barn where haystacks slept like big, shaggy dogs. The road climbed slightly, overlooking a field of tall grass, curving toward a tree-shaded pond where (I'm told) Thomas Merton used to write in a little toolshed overlooking the water.

I passed the pond and entered the woods—a young-growth forest of evergreen, sycamore, and sugar maple. The path led up a low ridge overlooking a grassy field. At one point the trail curved to the left again, and just beyond this bend stood a row of eastern pines—tall, gangly trees with sparse branches. They looked like stick men. One had been ravaged by a recent storm; it was twisted and split. It hadn't fallen, though—it clung together on one side while the rest was a tangle of splintered, white innards, like shredded meat. The tree leaned over a neighboring pine, and a wind made both of them move in a slow, steady rhythm.

I was struck by how human the whole scene looked, the tree like a fallen warrior being carried by a fellow soldier. And then I thought of Good Friday. I thought of Jesus, his flesh shredded by a Roman torturer. I thought of Simon of Cyrene carrying the cross when Jesus was too depleted to carry it any further. I thought of Jesus breathing his last, his body lowered from the cross by his family and friends.

I stood for a long, silent moment watching the shattered pine heave in the wind like slow, painful inhales and exhales. It felt as though the scene had been prepared for me—a larger-than-life Good Friday diorama. Then I saw myself in it. Ravaged, shattered, broken. I thought of my own failures and shortcomings, how impossible it would be for me to stuff my innards back in once torn open, how hopeless. But somehow, those needles remained green; life flowed through the broken tree.

I saw myself caught up and held together in the shattered body of Christ. Caught up in the life of one who somehow contains and conquers all of the world's darkness, ugliness, and brokenness, shielding us from even ourselves and making us new. Caught up in the life of a God who ended religion and freed me from ever having to prove myself again.

While most of us aren't tempted to worship clay idols or sacrifice animals, religious temptations nonetheless abound. The impulses toward self-made redemption we just explored capture our imaginations and draw us into a way of life. We display ourselves, seeking approval. We diet, exercise, and make cosmetic improvements in search of a better, more glorious self. We claw after power, success, and other symbols of our self-worth.

In contrast, the gospel invites us to lay down these efforts and trust wholly in the finished work of Jesus. It's a contrast of *do* versus *done* and an invitation to rest in the comfort and care of a merciful God who wants to bring us home. This is the defining story of the church, and the heart of its worship. How might we make it more central to daily life?

It may seem counterintuitive, but I believe that rooting ourselves in grace requires a deeper understanding of our need for grace.

A THREE-PART PRAYER

I want to suggest a practice that has its roots in the Prayer of Examen.

It's based on Paul's letter to the Corinthians where he said that Christians should examine their conscience before taking the Lord's Supper (1 Cor 11:28). Christians throughout the ages have practiced some version of it. The practice walks through a process of reflection: examining one's conscience and actions, paying attention to the ways that sin, idols, and selfish desires have hold of us.

It's a counterintuitive practice in our day and age, since the concept of sin is taboo. But as we look deep within ourselves, as we pay attention to the ways we've hurt others, fed addictions, and clung to our own self-redemptive efforts, we'll find that it not only deepens our awareness of the darkness within but also magnifies our vision for the grace God provides.

Over time, it will help us see patterns of selfishness and of running and hiding, and it will bring to light the things that we're trying to avoid—fear and anxiety, anger and bitterness, shame and sadness. It's a practice that isn't meant to burden us but to unburden us. It's meant for us to deal honestly with what's inside us, with what draws us away from God and the good life he offers, and so experience God's love and mercy in the deepest, darkest places.

The practice has three movements: examination, confession, and assurance.

Examination. We begin this way of prayer by examining ourselves. First you must sit quietly for a moment and pay attention to your mind and body. Are you angry? Bitter? Tense? Ashamed? Allow the feelings and emotions that come to the surface to inform you about the status of your own heart. Ask yourself why. Why are you mad? Why are you bitter? Why are you tired? See if any of your answers can be traced back to the religious impulses we just explored: Are you seeking self-justification (and failing to find it)? Are you struggling to display the "you" you want the world to see?

Ask God to open your mind and heart so that you might see anything that's offensive to him within you. From there, it's helpful to recount recent events. Think through the day, or recent days, and retrace your steps. What are your regrets? What do you wish you'd done differently? When did your emotions get away from you and why?

I find having my calendar in front of me with the events of the previous day laid out helpful in remembering where I was, who I encountered, and where my heart trafficked throughout the day.

Christians throughout the ages have encouraged this practice, coupling it with a meditation on the Ten Commandments, the seven deadly sins, or the Beatitudes. It's important to see these passages not merely as laws or rules but as invitations to a better way of life. Breaking the Ten Commandments is a sure path to dissatisfaction. Indulging in sin robs us of deeper joy. Life in the Beatitudes is a life liberated from the world and its petty gods.

Confession. As you search your heart, confess your sins. Be specific. I find a short litany to be helpful, simply praying, "Lord, in your mercy, hear my prayer. Forgive me for ____. Let me trust in Jesus' blood for forgiveness, and let me walk now by the light of the Holy Spirit." Then I continue my meditation on my days.

Assurance. End the practice by remembering that the work of grace is finished. Here, puritans like John Owen and Richard Baxter have great wisdom: we need to preach the gospel to ourselves. Jerry Bridges describes his version of the practice in *Respectable Sins*:

> Reliance on the twofold work of Christ for me is beautifully captured by Edward Mote in his hymn "The Solid Rock" with his words, "My hope is built on nothing less, than Jesus' blood and righteousness." Almost every day, I find myself going to those words in addition to reflecting on the promises of forgiveness in the Bible.
>
> What Scriptures do I use to preach the gospel to myself? Here are just a few I choose from each day:
>
> "As far as the east is from the west, so far does he remove our transgressions from us." (Psalm 103:12)

"I, I am he who blots out your transgressions for my own sake, and I will not remember your sins." (Isaiah 43:25)

"All we like sheep have gone astray; we have turned everyone one to his own way; and the LORD has laid on him the iniquity of us all." (Isaiah 53:6)

"Blessed are those whose lawless deeds are forgiven, and whose sins are covered; blessed is the man against whom the Lord will not count his sin." (Romans 4:7-8)[1]

Bridges goes on to say that as we reflect on these Scriptures and remember God's mercy, it's crucial that we look to Christ's reconciling work on the cross as the way that God has accomplished it.

Years ago, while on a retreat, Romans 8 wrecked me, exposing my lack of confidence in God's mercy and my grasping need to prove myself worthy. Romans 8:1 says simply, "There is therefore now no condemnation for those who are in Christ Jesus." Comfort could not be simpler or more explicit. What more needs to be done? What else can someone say once God—the judge— announces "no more condemnation"? I return to that verse often, and perhaps most often after a time of examination and confession.

The world around us wants to offer us a thousand cures for our spiritual anxiety. We can cover over those anxieties with veneer, we can devote ourselves to many different religious efforts, or we can stop all that effort altogether. We can look within and be honest about what's there and what we're trying to run away from or hide. And we can stand before the Lord with the confidence and comfort that comes from his mercy. To do so is one more step toward living in another world.

THREE

Selfie Sticks, Spectacles, and Sepulchers

The Old City of Jerusalem was hemmed in about five hundred years ago by massive limestone walls. Most of the city's sacred sites are inside. You enter through arched gateways, and inside, the cobbled streets are lined with shops and cafes. The scent lingers in my memory: the musty smell of an ancient city, meat grilling over hot coals, sweet-smelling tobacco burning on a hookah, citrus fruits and pomegranates being pressed into juices.

As you pass through the open-air shops, everything competes for your attention. Scarves and blocks of linen and quilts hanging in doorways. Shelves lined with white ceramics, each hand-painted in tiny geometric patterns of blue and yellow. A crowd of old men hunched around a backgammon game, slamming pieces on the board with meaty fists. Shopkeepers try to catch your eye and wave you inside. The crowd is a cross section of the Middle East: Jews and Arabs, Christians and Muslims, orthodox men with thick beards and heavy black clothing, women in headcoverings or hijabs. Soldiers who look like mere teenagers pass, M-16s draped over their shoulders. Police are everywhere. Loud scooters spewing exhaust weave their way through the pedestrians.

The Via Dolorosa—the "way of suffering" that Jesus walked from a Roman garrison to Golgotha—passes through the middle of all this. Narrow alleys and crowded streets lead to a doorway that opens up into the courtyard of the Church of the Holy Sepulchre—the site of both Golgotha and the empty tomb. The courtyard is usually swarming with tourists and pilgrims. Tour guides wear headset microphones like Britney Spears, with speakers on lanyards around their necks. They carry brightly colored little golf flags to rally their groups, and they recite scripts about the history of the church in English, German, Korean, and more.

The church itself is austere. Grey stone, blunt medieval arches. It was originally built in the fourth century, and it's been knocked down and restored several times over.

Inside, a winding staircase leads to the shrine built around the spot where, tradition holds, the cross actually stood. The staircase is packed and the line moves slowly. Anxious pilgrims push past while you wait. At the top, the shrine is ornate and gilded, with candles burning everywhere. Lamps hang from the ceiling and let out a flickering light through amber and red glass. Priests direct traffic, offering blessings. Pilgrims press in and line up to kneel at the spot where the cross stood, to touch it, to bless themselves.

I wondered what it must be like to be one of those priests, standing there for hours a day, several days a week, managing the crowd like a ride operator at Epcot.

On my first visit, I avoided the line and wandered toward the back, taking the whole scene in. I found myself near the exit with a perfect vantage to watch the faces of people as they left the altar. I'll never forget the face of a young Russian woman as she passed. She was beautiful, like a femme fatale in a Bond movie. She wore stark makeup and slickly styled hair. Her companion matched her, looking like a Bond villain's henchman. He was huge and muscled, wearing a skin-tight white t-shirt and tattered jeans and heavy boots. Stone-faced, arm around her, he guided her through the crowd. She was falling apart. Tears streaming, nose running, streaks of mascara running down her face. She gasped for air and wept bitterly after touching the disc that marks the spot where Jesus died. I watched her pass and wondered why I felt so detached, wondered if I should get in the line to touch the disc.

A little further into the church you'll find a marble slab called the Stone of the Anointing. It's the same color as the peach and pink terrazzo floors of the high school I attended twenty years ago. According to tradition, it held Jesus' body in the tomb. It's set into the floor, marked off by tall brass candleholders and big frosted glass lanterns embossed with gold crosses. I saw an old woman wearing a shawl over her head press through the crowd with force. She knelt at the stone and opened a plastic shopping bag, stacking little neon yellow crosses and tacky plastic rosaries on the marble. She prayed rapidly and mechanically, rubbing the stone with each cross before shoving it back into the plastic bag. The bag crinkled loudly.

I have a butcher-block island in my kitchen. We leave it unfinished and use it as a cutting board and prep area for cooking. Over time, it gets stained with berries and vinegar, or with the *jus* from a roast. Once a year or so, I'll sand it down, just a little, to strip out the stains and leave it clean and smooth again. I thought about that butcher block as I watched this lady rub the little plastic crosses on the marble stone like she was trying to shave away something and take it with her.

Still further into the church you'll find the Aedicule. This is the site of Jesus' tomb and was once buried in a hillside. The Emperor

Constantine ordered the hill removed and the tomb enclosed and protected within the church. Today, you walk into a gorgeous grey rotunda surrounding a squat brown hut. The hut itself is adorned with gold and red velvet and brass candles. The line to enter the Aedicule and see the tomb stood about eight people wide and wrapped all the way around the shrine. To get in, one had to wait an hour or more.

All around crowds shuffled past. Guides chattered loudly through their little speakers. Person after person would try to see the tomb, standing on their tiptoes to peek over the crowd and catch a glimpse of the gilded room inside. Several people stood near the entrance, raised a selfie stick in the air, and snapped a photo. Some looked serious (as serious as one can look while holding something as ridiculous as a selfie stick), but most made typical selfie faces: wide-open-mouth smiles, heads tilted, arms around their companions. Some threw up peace signs. More than one made a duck face.

The crowd in the line at the Aedicule would sometimes smile and wave as though there was nothing disjointed about taking selfies in the Church of the Holy Sepulchre.

One would think that standing in one of Christianity's most sacred sites would be a breathtaking, moving experience. But for me it felt strange. I felt a sincere desire to connect to the place, to acknowledge the history and commemorate it while I was there, but I also felt distant. Resistant. The touristy nature of the place is partly to blame, but something within me *wanted* to keep it at a distance.

I'm sure anyone's visit here will feel disjointed. The crowd itself is disjointed—the heartbroken woman at Golgotha, the woman at the Stone of the Anointing, and the teenager making a duckface at a selfie stick in front of the empty tomb. But there is also a gap between the kind of devotion this place invites and my own religious posture. I'm wired to resist. Trained.

For some of the church's visitors, the place remains *enchanted*. Those visitors enter with a sense of spiritual possibility that others do not. They are open to the possibility of sacred spaces and sacred objects. I enter with a sense of distance and suspicion.

This isn't to say there isn't good reason for some of that suspicion. Even at my best and most spiritual moments, I wouldn't advocate trying to spiritually supercharge plastic crosses by rubbing them on a sacred marble stone.

But it seems like somewhere between the superstitious world of supercharged neon crosses and the disenchanted world of selfie-takers, there is a way of being that allows for spiritual possibilities, for God's presence, and for the possibility of sacred space. Unfortunately, my spiritual upbringing did not prepare me to live in that world.

I grew up in evangelical churches and was raised on a steady diet of spectacle and hype. When I was six or seven, I was in a Christmas musical at a megachurch in Houston. My memories of it are a little fuzzy, but I believe it was a "Christmas Through the Years" sort of thing, with each musical number representing how the holiday may have been celebrated in a given decade. They sang "Rockin' Around the Christmas Tree" for the fifties and "I'll Be Home for Christmas" for the forties, all in vaguely decade-appropriate costumery.

My number was set in the sixties. I wore white bell-bottoms that had a triangle of silk polka-dotted fabric in the bells, a baggy orange satin tunic, and love beads. On the night we tried on our costumes, another kid dropped his pants in the toilet and tried to pretend like nothing happened; he just handed back dripping pants to the costumers.

We sang and danced to "Do-Re-Mi" from *The Sound of Music*, which I believe is as close to psychedelia as the Baptist music minister was willing to get. A lady named Sherri, who wore enough makeup to look like a rodeo clown, played Maria. At the dress rehearsal, they recorded her voice for the performance; she would be lip-synching. To my mind, this was a horrific lie, but convictions about artistic integrity from a six-or-seven-year-old went unheard. I am not certain what long-term psychological trauma this all caused.

A few months before this, I got baptized at a different Baptist megachurch in Houston. In my memories, this place shares the size and aesthetics of a convention center. Massive, modern, and cold. The pastor who baptized me put on heavy rubber waders, fixed his hair in a mirror, slid a white robe over his shoulders, and fixed his hair again. He politely asked those of us getting baptized that we try not to splash his hair when we got in and out of the water.

That same pastor now has his own church, spread across several states, where they show his sermons on big video screens. I hear they film him with RED cameras, which cost about as much as a house. He has a blog about pastors' fashion and he endorsed men's Spanx. He wrote a book about sex and spent a day and a night broadcasting interviews about it from a bed on the roof of his church. He also has rap videos on YouTube. I am not making any of this up.

Later, we moved from Houston to New Albany, Indiana, and it wasn't long before I made it to the youth group. Though it was led by sincere, kind, and goodhearted people, it was also strange. Spectacle and hype were certainly its breath and bread.

Weekly gatherings were punctuated by games like Chubby Bunny and Honey, If You Love Me, You'll Smile. The former is innocuous enough: you stuff your face with marshmallows and attempt to say the phrase "chubby bunny." The person who can fit the most marshmallows in their mouth and still get the words out wins. There was nearly always vomiting, and urban legends swirled about some kid who died while playing the game.

The latter was slightly more sinister. In this game, if you're "it," you have to approach a person of the opposite sex and say, "Honey, if you love me, you'll smile." They must reply, "Honey, I love you, but I just can't smile." You get three chances to make the person break by smiling or laughing, and then you must move on to someone else. Typically, winning was accomplished with techniques that bordered on sexual harassment.

That wasn't the worst, though. The worst was Red Grass, a game we played at camp in Northern Indiana. Thirty gallon plastic trashcans were filled with a thick, overly concentrated mix of red Kool-Aid and had giant straws placed in them. Teams were formed, and the first team to empty their Kool-Aid can by drinking (or sucking and spitting) all of the Kool-Aid from their can was the big winner. Mind you, this is all taking place in triple-digit summer heat.

Kids, sweating profusely, drank as much as they could, ran a short distance, and barfed the nearly fluorescent red sludge into the grass ("Red Grass" being more than just a clever name). Once they recovered, they'd return to the trash can and repeat the cycle.

By the end, the scene had a Jonestown-Massacre-like quality to it. Kids staggered around, dazed. Some lay in patches of dry grass, heaving. The air was thick with the smell of fruit punch and the vinegary odor of vomit. The game was later banned. Like Chubby Bunny, rumors swirled that some kid died while playing it.

Hype extended far beyond these games and into our spiritual experiences. At youth groups, camps, and retreats, most of the speakers were young men in their twenties and thirties who, in hindsight, all remind me of Dane Cook. I remember one conference that ended with a clip from the movie *Glory*. It was a scene before the last battle in the film, where Matthew Broderick asks who will carry the flag if the standard bearer falls during a charge into battle. This was used as a metaphor. "The flag of our faith has fallen," he said. "Who will stand to carry it into the next generation?" There was a pregnant pause, and then, in the back of the room, a brave soul yelled, "I will." Soon, the whole auditorium rumbled with shuffling feet and the folding of the heavy theater seats as kids all over the room stood and shouted, "I will." It was moving. I think I teared up.

The next year at this same conference, this gag was repeated, only instead of *Glory*, the video clip was the "Oh Captain, My Captain" scene in *Dead Poets Society*. My friend Lachlan leaned over and said, "He's going to make us all stand up." Sure enough, after some set up, there was a pregnant pause, and "Oh Captain, My Captain!" Shuffling feet. Everyone who hadn't attended the year before was deeply moved.

The next year, it repeated again.

Between these moments were countless others spent huddled in small groups, friends' homes, or cars, where we talked more plainly and quietly about our faith. These moments weren't without depth or sincerity, but they were peripheral. They were in the margins. They came without much guidance or instruction. Rarely did someone sit down to talk to us about the daily, mundane aspects of faith. It didn't fit the logic of everything else they told us about faith: being a Christian was too *awesome!* to be ordinary. So I was trained to live from one pyrotechnic moment to the next, one hyped up emotional mountain to another.

My experience was tame compared to what many Christians have seen and experienced in churches. There are countless examples of faith healers, snake-handlers, and extreme charismatic happenings like holy laughter, holy barking, and more.

A more recent oddity was the glory cloud manifestations that happened at Bethel Church in Redding, California. Over a period of several months during worship services at the church, a glitter cloud appeared in the air over the heads of worshipers while they were singing, dancing, and crying out for God to appear. People reported seeing jewels show up on the carpet or even in their homes after they left the church. Pilgrims made the journey to Bethel to see the glory cloud and enroll in their School of Supernatural Ministry.[1]

A friend of mine attended one of these services. As the cloud appeared at this particular service, it was accompanied by feathers, which folks (naturally?) assumed were angel feathers. My friend was watching a feather fall toward him when an ecstatic young girl pushed him out of the way, opened her arms to the sky, and caught the feather in her mouth. She ate it.

You can watch scenes like this on YouTube. You can also see several videos that analyze the phenomenon, including folks who look at the stuff under a microscope. It turns out the dust from the glory cloud looks an awful lot like the kind of cosmetic body glitter favored by cheerleaders and strippers. It also turns out that the cloud's point of entry into the room is near the church's HVAC vents.

As Spinal Tap's Nigel Tufnel once said, "There's a fine line between clever and stupid." More to the point, there's a fine line between wanting to cultivate an emotionally transcendent experience and pumping stripper glitter into the air vents. And while religious hoaxes are as old as humanity itself, there's a thread that connects this one to Red Grass, to emotionally manipulative church gatherings, and to every other hype-and-spectacle phenomenon in the church today. All are rooted in a deep cynicism.

They reveal a loss of confidence in the practices that have formed and united the church for generations before—practices rooted in word, prayer, and song, habits that celebrate the covenantal, shared life of a faith community. If we have no confidence that God is going to show up in these practices, then we have one mandate: *make something happen.*

I don't think my experience is atypical. For many who grew up in North American evangelicalism, what I just described should sound fairly normal. What was regular about church (regular in the sense of repeated regularly) was the way it strove for the heights. A good worship experience involved emotional catharsis, ending with tears and bold commitments. Ordinariness, as a whole, was shunned in favor of being radical, extreme, and so forth.

I remember one church camp where the preacher rebuked this pattern of lunging from one mountaintop experience to the next. A steady diet of emotional highs was no way to live a faithful Christian life, he said. And yet he preached this in a context where over the course of a day we were once again whipped into a frenzy, marched to an actual hilltop, and called to make big commitments. The irony is not unlike a scene at the end of *PCU* where the troublemakers on a college campus rebuke a politically correct mob for protesting everything. The mob responds by breaking out signs and marching, chanting, "We're not gonna protest!"

Mountaintop moments create their own normality. We learn to depend on them, and we feel starved when they're removed. We might find ourselves in the Church of the Holy Sepulchre unable to connect with the place. Where's the motivational speech? Where's the rock band? Who's going to help me *feel* something?

The power of habit is in the way it tunes our body and soul to anticipate a return to the rhythm. We're primed for it, and when we're starved of it, we'll feel pangs of hunger.

This way of thinking about our habits is even more interesting when compared with the ancient church. Historically, the church cultivated habits and disciplines that oriented people to the faith through the practices of liturgy—regularly praying the Psalms, reciting the creed, celebrating the Lord's Supper, baptizing and catechizing converts—and the church calendar—Advent to Christmas, Lent to Easter, and many other feasts and celebrations between.

> Chasing religious spectacles only makes sense in a disenchanted world.

Many Christian churches have moved away from these rhythms of life, and not always for bad reasons. The last hundred and fifty years of Christianity in the West have been a strange cocktail of theological erosion (the slide into liberalism) and reaction (the nervous hedging of fundamentalism). Some churches with good traditions like those listed above weren't immune to theological erosion, and while their practices continued to display and proclaim the gospel, their core beliefs refuted it. Others threw the baby out with the bathwater, rejecting practices and traditions they associated with liberalism, empty traditions, or superstition.

At the same time, revivalism was thriving. In place of the church's liturgy, revivalistic worship services consisted of a lengthy period of singing and a sermon that called for repentance and recommitment. This formula "worked." It led to many, many conversions and rededications, and in most corners of North American evangelicalism, it's still the model for our modern worship services.

The gap between these ways of gathering isn't just an issue for church leaders. It reveals something much deeper about the Christian life. The traditional way the church approached spiritual formation is embedded in those older practices: the movements of the liturgy, the broad readings of the lectionary, the seasons of lament like Advent and Lent. The church immersed believers in a way of life that regularly rehearsed the gospel and taught them to cry out to God in the midst of suffering and disappointment.

In place of this is a revivalistic spirit that aims for knockout punches: worship gatherings, retreats, and conferences that hinge on big moments, big decisions, big commitments. But the need for hype crowds out our darkness, sadness, and lament. Pastors end up sounding like Margaret Cho's portrayal of Kim Jong Il on *30 Rock*, declaring that as Christians, it's "always sunny here, all the time."

Before we lay all the blame on pastors, let's at least ask whether the problem is one of supply or demand. Are church leaders emphasizing positivity and spectacle because they want to attract followers and sell them religious snake oil? Or are they emphasizing positivity and spectacle because that's what the church is demanding? I think it's a combination of both. Like the passengers on the train in *Murder on the Orient Express*, (spoiler alert) we all did it. We can't just blame leaders. We all live in search of big cathartic moments.

Chasing religious spectacles only makes sense in a disenchanted world. If we've primed ourselves to live in a world where God doesn't show up, then we have to figure out how to make something happen on our own. We need (to borrow Bart Simpson's description of contemporary worship) "Lights, Smoke, and Tae Bo!"

Standing in the Aedicule, watching pilgrims pass by, feeling alien, I wondered, how much has my sense of transcendence and understanding of the practice of Christianity been shackled to these cultural trappings? How far removed from ordinary life is it? Is it strange that I can be brought to tears when I'm in my church and someone plays a song describing the death of Jesus or the nativity, but when I stand in the actual places these events happened, I feel so awkward, so resistant, so removed?

I can critique the woman with the neon crosses all I want. It's easy to see how much she resembles the feather-eating girl standing below the glory cloud. But I also see how much she resembles me. I am just as culturally conditioned, just as hooked on spectacle and hype, which is to say, just as superstitious.

There's a common thread between these experiences. All of our religious efforts grow from hearts that long for redemption, for transcendence, and that most of all long to connect with God. So we look for him in enchanted objects, like plastic crosses or feathers from heaven, or we look for him to meet us in the climactic moments of a worship service.

More than anything, we're looking for some kind of assurance that God is still there, that he'll still show up for us in life and death. To find that assurance, we have to separate what we've become habituated to expect—mountaintop experiences of varying kinds—and what he promises—the quiet comfort of his real presence.

In the Scriptures we see that he comes not in a storm, but in a still, small voice. Not in a conquering hero, but a carpenter. Not in a victorious tribe, but in an impoverished and persecuted church. The real wonder is that this is what we really want. The mountaintop experiences don't satisfy, but the presence of Jesus does, and he's promised that he won't forsake us.

He's as present when we're mowing the lawn or arguing with our boss as

> The mountaintop experiences don't satisfy, but the presence of Jesus does, and he's promised that he won't forsake us.

he is at an altar call or in our quiet moments of prayer. It's mysterious and hidden, and yet it's a core promise of the New Testament: God is with us.

We'll need to learn to differentiate our sense of that presence from the excitement that comes at a hyped-up worship service. We'll need to discover that his presence is often much simpler, quieter, and more subtle than our experiences in church have trained us to believe.

This isn't to say that joyful, ecstatic moments aren't important. We need them. We need moments when the seas part, when the mountains smolder, and when the dead rise. But we also need God's presence in an ordinary way, in the steady guidance of a cloud by day and a fire by night. We need lamplight for our steps and the nearness and lowliness of a shepherd. And we need confidence in that presence when storms come and suffering leaves us weary and sad—the dark nights at bedsides and in hospitals when the last thing that would comfort us is a rockin' worship set with lasers and smoke.

Only that kind of presence is a ballast against suffering and doubt. Only that kind of presence can allow us to grow deep roots in a disenchanted world. It's a presence we come to know most intimately in the quietness of prayer and in the simplicity of God's word. A spirituality that doesn't teach us to pray in our darkest hours or doesn't teach us to listen to God's voice through Scripture is going to leave us starving and searching for something more.

In the days after my visit to the church, a tension opened up inside me. The longer I stayed in Jerusalem, the more ordinary the place became. These are streets like many cities' streets, and people who are like any other—warm, human, broken.

And yet, on a stone in the midst of it, the greatest mystery in creation took place. The Son of God hung and died for me, pouring out grace that was powerful enough to reconcile the whole world to its Creator.

He bled on a dull, grey limestone rock. His body was covered in the sweat and dust from these ordinary streets. It was not the gilded beauty of Jerusalem's holy places that caught my imagination and finally stirred my heart; it was its ordinariness.

On our last day in Jerusalem, my wife and I returned to the Church of the Holy Sepulchre. We walked through the Old City's narrow streets again, past the silks, the clouds of tobacco smoke, the rotating stands draped with rosaries and crosses and olive wood trinkets, back to the crowded courtyard and into the medieval building. This time, though, we wandered back behind the shrine of Golgotha, down the steps into the chapel of St. Helena.

St. Helena was the mother of the Emperor Constantine, and the chapel is one of the oldest remaining structures of the original third-century church. The stone walls along the steps are carved with primitive graffiti crosses, the work of medieval pilgrims. The floor is a gorgeous Byzantine mosaic, and the chapel's altar keeps an enshrined piece of the original cross—or so tradition holds.

A guide passed through with a small group of tourists as we stood there looking at the mosaic floor. He pointed out the chapel's features, the floor, the relic, and the graffiti. Then he pointed to the limestone wall to our right—a raw grey-white rock face that was partially covered in thick plexiglass. "This, of course, is also Golgotha—and this is one of the few sections of the rock that's exposed." The crowd nodded, snapped a few photos, and moved on, leaving Sarah and me alone in the chapel.

I was fixated on that rock face. Buddy Miller's song "Fall on the Rock" played in my head. I tried to wrap my mind around the fact that there, on that rock, God incarnate shed his blood. Not some abstract or metaphorical rock, but this one, this piece of stone right in front of me. I walked over to the wall, feeling uncomfortable and strange as I looked at the rock face. Finally, I reached out and touched the stone.

Nothing extraordinary happened as I stood there with my hand against the wall. I just closed my eyes and took a deep breath and felt the strangeness of the world and the incomprehensibility of this place that enshrines death and resurrection and that draws pilgrims from the world over and has for almost two thousand years. I thought about the quaking earth and torn curtain, the forsakenness of the Son and the emptiness of the tomb. I thought about bread and wine and body and blood and a church that proclaims this death "until he returns." Never has hype or spectacle seemed more absurd. Who needs a greater drama than death, resurrection, and scandalous grace? Poetry and art and a lifetime of prayer and reflection can only begin to explore this wild story, something we hope is true though the world rolls its eyes and tries desperately to drain the magic out of it.

I stood there, fingers pressed to a wall worn smooth by the hands of a thousand pilgrims, touching the rock where the most important thing in the world happened. My doubts were there, too, circling like hungry sharks, ready to strike when my thoughts presented the slightest of openings. I breathed deep, held still, and prayed, "My God, it did happen." In a way, I feel like I've been leaning there ever since.

PATHWAY 3
BRINGING SCRIPTURE TO LIFE

I think much of our hunger for spectacle and hype comes from a lack of imagination. To find ourselves captivated by the Christian life and captivated by the Scriptures requires an active mind and an engaged imagination. It's the imagination that brings this world to life.

I've wondered if this is because of laziness: it's much easier to keep people engaged with noise and lights. But I think it's mostly because of a lack of training and a lack of practice. Like learning to read or speak, we have to learn to imagine. It takes practice, and it requires that we're willing to work with what we have at the beginning—a diminished imagination—and let it grow.

The title of this pathway has a double meaning. It means first that we want to reawaken our imaginations to the Bible. We want to enter its world and see it as more than mere facts or words on a page. It means second that we want to bring it to our lives, to fill our world with its words.

Much that falls into the category of Bible study these days can serve to keep Scriptures at a distance. (I've talked about this already a bit in chapter one.) We anatomize Scripture, breaking it down into component pieces and categories, but we struggle to see it as a whole. And if this is all we know of the Bible, it's no wonder we gravitate toward spectacle. Scripture itself remains lifeless and dead.

But while the modern impulse is to study the Bible like one might study gypsy moths or cheese mold, previous generations treated the Bible as a living thing. Rather than merely being a text we illuminate with the tools of historical research, analysis, and deconstruction, it can be a lamplight, illuminating our world.

To that end, I want to suggest a couple of practices that reorient our approach to the Bible, aiming at the imagination and the heart. For many Christians, these practices will feel at least a little strange because they invite us to approach the Bible in a much different way than we're used to.

IGNATIAN PRAYER

Ignatius of Loyola taught his followers to read the Gospels with an active imagination. Hear the story of Jesus healing a paralytic or talking with the woman at the well, and imagine yourself in the story, encountering Jesus, hearing his healing words as if he were saying them to you. Hear it as if you were the paralytic or as if you were a bystander. Feel the heat of the sun, the weariness of a journey on a long road, the shame of sin and exposure, the judgment and condemnation from religious professionals, and imagine Jesus. What might he sound like? Does he touch you as he passes? Does he look you in the eyes? What do you hear? What do you feel?

Scripture is living. It's meant to take root, growing and flowering in the heart and mind. Don't just know what the story says; know how it feels, explore what the characters in the story must have experienced when they encountered Jesus, or saw the seas part, or watched Lazarus stroll out of an empty tomb picking gauze off his newly-animated skin. The point is not to turn the Bible into a *Choose Your Own Adventure* story but to let the Bible speak with a richness we often deny it.

How to practice it. This may sound obvious, but go somewhere where you can avoid interruption.

Set a timer. This allows you to not worry about how long you should go or when you're done. Put your phone on do not disturb, and put the timer out of view. When the bell rings, you're done. Initially, you should aim small—just a few minutes (3–5)—but as you get more comfortable with it, add a few minutes at a time.

Practices like this should have a beginning, middle, and end—a routine that your mind and body learn and can easily step into. Begin by taking a moment to calm down your mind and body. Sit in a chair, or kneel on the floor, and open your Bible. Pray a short breath prayer a few times.

Take a short passage from one of the Gospels, such as any of the stories in Matthew 8. Read the passage a couple of times and allow your imagination to start filling in the details: the scenery, the weather, the sounds in the background, the smell of the sea or (less pleasant) the smell of the leprous beggar. Imagine the nervous expression on the face of the centurion.

After a couple of readings, let your mind wander into that world. Focus on senses: sight, smell, sound, touch, taste.

When the timer goes off, take another moment to pray and reflect. What struck you? What part of the story might be worth coming back to later in the day?

This practice gets richer with repetition. You're training your mind to imagine, and in doing so, you're liberating yourself from the need for spectacle and external stimulation.

PRAYING THE PSALMS

The second practice that can help the Bible enter our lives is praying the Psalms. The monastic tradition of chanting through the Psalms in regular rhythms throughout the day provides a sharp contrast to our world of on-demand everything, where streaming content can immediately satisfy our appetites and next-day or same-day delivery provides access to everything from books to clothes to dog houses. In the practice of praying the hours, as Benedictine sister Joan Chittister once put it, we don't pray because we feel like it, and we don't even pray because of what we hope to get out of it—communion with God or peace for our souls. Instead, we pray "because the bell rings."[1] We pray because we've chosen to orient our life around prayer, and we submit ourselves wholly to that life. Rather than our spiritual life being reactive—constantly responding to life's circumstances—this way of life is a steady rhythm and an anchor. Rather than trying to find words to express whatever we might be experiencing, we pray the Scriptures and try to find our lives in those words.

There are many, ways to adapt this practice to our ordinary life. To start, one might simply adopt what Donald Whitney calls the psalm of the day.[2] In this method, you take whatever day of the month it is and add thirty to it four times. So if it's the first of the month, your psalms are 1, 31, 61, 91, and 121. Open your Bible to the first psalm on the list and start reading. If it doesn't seem to speak to where you are at that time, jump to the next one, and so on, until you find a Psalm that feels like an invitation. Then, simply let the words of the Psalm guide your prayers.

How to practice it. Like the Ignatian prayer method described above, I think having an intentional beginning, middle, and end helps to make something like this a habit. So, as described above: set a timer, start with a few breath prayers to calm your mind and body, and begin praying the psalm.

I love the way Dr. Whitney simplifies this kind of prayer. Wherever your mind goes as you read and pray, let it go. Offer those thoughts up to God. If the word "cypress" shows up, and you're reminded of a friend named Cypress, pray for Cypress. There's not a right and wrong way to practice this kind of prayer. This isn't the time or place to think too hard about the psalm itself, but rather to let the psalm be your guide. You're bringing your life into the text and, through the text, to God.

Once either of these practices becomes a habit, you might consider practicing it a few times a day—a longer meditation in the morning and perhaps a short meditation in the evening, or at lunchtime, wherever you can make the space. Don't feel like you have to go for hours and hours to make it meaningful. Instead, think of it like the bells at a monastery, a break in the current of your day that calls your mind and heart back to the kingdom of God, and an invitation to reframe the day in light of that kingdom. All it takes is a few minutes. Set a reminder on a clock or a smartphone for 11:30 in the morning, or for 8:00 at night, and when you hear the bell, pray.

These two practices train us to bring our imaginations and our hearts into the text. Ignatian prayer helps us connect to Scripture as a story and to its characters as real, ordinary people. Praying the Psalms gives us language to pray wholehearted and earthy prayers with a wide and deep emotional range. Together, they help us experience the Bible not as a textbook, and not as a corpse, but as living, breathing words. In practicing these types of prayer, we not only lose our taste for distraction-filled spectacles, we might just help to re-enchant our world.

FOUR

Solitude and Secrecy

Every summer I take my family down to the Florida panhandle for our vacation. While I'm there I try to wake up at sunrise and go for a run, tracing a few miles of the hard-packed sand that the surf rolls smooth as it laps in and out. It's the perfect time to be on the beach. It's mostly empty, and you can feel the air change as the sun rises. Pelicans fly in impossibly low formation above the surf, and occasionally dolphins and sand sharks can be seen rolling on the surface, feeding on the pompano that run between the sand bars near the shore.

A few years ago, after a run, I was walking back toward town, crossing the dunes on a wood-plank walkover. Some bushes just to my right began to stir, and a moment later a fox leapt from them onto the walkover, calm as she could be. She was lean and lithe and wild, red as a glowing ember, and when she moved you could see the layers in her fur—her sandy undercoat, the dark tips of fur near her ankles and the tips of her ears. Her tail was enormous and hailed a warning, like someone waving a mace.

She stood ten or fifteen feet away and stared at me. There was no one else around. She didn't bristle. She wasn't startled. But she did pause. When her eyes met mine, I felt like I was looking into something I would never really comprehend. Something both fierce and frail. Something that shared my creatureliness but whose own nature was so vastly different from mine as to be incomprehensible. She too is dust. She too is fearfully and wonderfully made. But aside from knowing that, she is a mystery.

She turned and never looked my way again, disappearing into the dunes, silent as a ghost.

That happened just a few years ago. If it happened today, I can imagine it being different. There'd be an additional layer of temptation. Back then, I wasn't on Facebook or Twitter. I doubt I even had a camera on my phone, and if I did, its resolution would have been laughable by today's standards. Today I'd be tempted to grab my phone and take a picture. Rather than standing face-to-face with the wild, I'd be mediating the moment through my phone.

It's a pervasive temptation these days. You can't go anywhere without finding yourself surrounded by people with smartphones and tablets, capturing photos and video of everything from dinner at Applebee's to movies and concerts. While on an anniversary trip with my wife a couple of years ago, we went to a traditional Hawaiian Luau. In the middle of the show, a woman at a table in front of us stood up with a full-sized iPad, capturing video of the fire dancers, oblivious to the fact that she was blocking the view of dozens of people behind her. It's the first time I can remember seeing someone use something as clumsy as an iPad to capture photos. Now I see it all the time. Jack White sometimes opens his concerts with a plea for everyone to put their phones away and simply experience the show—a request that is usually mostly ignored. Louis CK tells fans he meets in public that he won't take a picture with them, but he will talk to them. Some people are satisfied, but many walk away angry and frustrated.[1] I suspect that it's because they weren't after the opportunity to meet Louis—they wanted to be able to *show people* they met Louis.

I've seen parents post Facebook updates for every moment of their potty training adventures, including photos of diaper blowouts. Keep in mind that these photos are now online, and we have no reason to believe they won't be there when said child turns fifteen or is running for office at fifty.

The spiritual life is not immune to this culture of display. We Instagram photos from church gatherings and worship services, tweet quotes from sermons and books we're reading, and we share the old-fashioned way too: we talk. We talk endlessly about what we're learning, what we're struggling with, and what we're doing in hopes of spiritual growth. This temptation has always existed, but now it's available in cut-and-paste memes.

I treasure the encounter I had with the fox, and I treasure the memory of it that I get to keep. In hindsight, reaching for my phone would have been vulgar. Instead of what I experienced—a moment standing face-to-face with the wild—I would instead have a memory of me fumbling with my phone. That's the dirty secret of social media; we can't capture a moment without molesting it first. We introduce a mediator for our experience. Instead of an encounter between me and the fox, it would have been me, the fox, and my phone.

I remember another moment on that same trip, gathered with some friends while our kids played King of the Hill on some dunes by the beach. "Get your phone," one friend said to her husband as the kids tumbled over the dunes. "No," he replied, "I want to do this in analog; I want to remember it."

Hannah Arendt wrote, "A life spent entirely in public, in the presence of others, becomes, as we would say, shallow. While it retains its visibility, it loses the quality of rising into sight from some darker ground which must remain hidden if it is not to lose its depth in a very real, non-subjective sense."[2] Arendt wrote these words in 1958, in a world that was far less connected than ours. Nonetheless, she saw a trajectory—a tendency toward constant social activity and a demand from the public to be perpetually entertained. To Arendt, this was not only causing the evaporation of privacy and solitude but the evaporation of the space to think and reflect. If only she could see us now.

When are we ever truly alone?

Jesus' life was marked as much by withdrawal as by engagement. After his baptism, he disappeared into the desert for forty days. Throughout his ministry, he returned to solitude. He withdrew to mourn the death of John the Baptist. Mark and Luke both describe him rising early and seeking "desolate places." On the night before his crucifixion, he went to the garden of Gethsemane with the twelve and left even them to go and pray alone.

This pattern of withdrawal doesn't mark Jesus as a special case and isn't a reflection of his divinity. Instead, it's a perfect expression of his humanity. A body has limited resources, and what we do each day depletes those resources: our physical energy, our psychological energy, our

> Jesus' life was marked as much by withdrawal as by engagement.

capacity for empathy, and even our capacity to make decisions.[3] Jesus, incarnate and embodied, experienced these limits. Just as he needed food and oxygen and sleep, he needed solitude. Saying this doesn't accuse Jesus of a flaw or an imperfection. Instead, it points out that being perfectly human means being contingent—requiring food and rest and solitude in order to live perfectly. Humanity isn't limitless and self-sufficient but deeply dependent on God's provision.

We often imagine a perfect human as invulnerable to weakness. Superman, vulnerable on his own planet, is empowered by the light of our sun so that he is essentially indestructible. He doesn't tire. He doesn't require food or water. So long as he takes in the sun's rays, he is, well, super. Similarly, we often liken high-performance athletes to machines or beasts. Note, though, that this language dehumanizes them.

Far from being invulnerable and superhuman, Jesus is truly and deeply human. He is vulnerable to hunger and weariness. He is vulnerable to fear and anxiety, as the blood, sweat, and tears of Gethsemane demonstrate. He is perfect not because he never tires of the crowd and the work of ministry but because he rightly responds to weariness, withdrawing to desolate places to rest and pray. This is the hidden ground from which his ministry arises.

Notice that when the devil came to tempt Jesus, he only came after Jesus had spent forty days in solitude. Some read this and think the devil was being opportunistic, attacking Jesus only after the pressures of the desert and fasting had weakened him. I don't think that's true. Unbeknownst to the devil, he tempted the Son not at his weakest but at his strongest. He was not tempted by bread because for forty days, he'd learned to live without it. Likewise, the adoration of the crowds and the lust for power had no appeal either.

There's a romanticized view of solitude that's often expressed among Christians. We think if we had the time and space to withdraw for a while, we'd experience peace and bliss. But the reality is often much more harsh and difficult. In solitude, we seek God, but the first thing we encounter is ourselves. The real you shows up, with all of its embarrassing attributes. Frustrated about your sex life? Tired of compulsively eating garbage? Burdened by the shame of an addiction to pornography or substances? Solitude often forces us to look these sorrows square in the face and makes us reckon with a cold reality: we like our busyness. We like the chaos of our lives. We like it because it distracts us from ourselves.

Solitude has a learning curve. It's a practice we embody, and like anything worth doing, our first efforts will be pained. The "terror of silence" (as David Foster Wallace called it) will tempt us away from the quiet. We will long for email, to-do lists, a sink full of dishes, the unread messages on our phone—anything that can turn our attention away from that quietly simmering something that makes solitude so troubling.

So we practice solitude like a beginning violinist; we practice poorly. But poor practice—marked by a wandering and restless mind—isn't bad practice. Done with some regularity, it can become rich. We can discover a space in our hearts and in our world where the Lord meets us. As we'll see, it's the beginning of the end of our religious efforts, a chance to face both the reality of our spiritual poverty and the wealth of God's spiritual blessings.

The Bible often likens God's relationship to his people to that of a lover. God is the Lover; we are his Beloved. Lovers share more than their physical intimacy; they share their secrets, their pasts, their desires and disappointments. Nothing will end a relationship more quickly than betrayal of that confidence. We need a space for similar intimacy with God. We need a space in our life for stories and experiences that exist only between him and us.

So we need to guard the borders of our solitude with another discipline—one the church has called the practice of secrecy. There need to be aspects of our spiritual life that are kept intimate and private, between us and God alone.

Henri Nouwen likens the spiritual life to keeping a fire in a hearth in a small cottage. When the door is closed, the fire warms the whole space. Whenever the door opens, the heat escapes, and eventually, the whole room cools. There are times to open the door, times to share and invite others to know what we've learned and experienced, but they are the exception, not the rule. In a world of constant display, many of us have never closed the door at all. Every spiritual experience is something we try to share and broadcast. Every moment of silence is interrupted by noise, by messages, and by the presence of others. We long for more depth and more intimacy, but we don't realize the small ways we are draining it out of our lives.

When Jesus taught his disciples to pray, he said,

> And when you pray, you must not be like the hypocrites. For they love to stand and pray in the synagogues and at the street corners, that they may be seen by others. Truly, I say to you, they have received their reward. But when you pray, go into your room and shut the door and pray to your Father who is in secret. And your Father who sees in secret will reward you. (Mt 6:5-6)

There need to be aspects of our spiritual life that are kept intimate and private, between us and God alone.

The impulse to live our spiritual lives on display is, clearly, nothing new. Jesus warns us that living this way means we "have our reward." If you're praying because you want to be esteemed by the people who see you pray, that's all the benefit you'll receive. If you want to seek God, you must go and pray "in secret."

Jesus both embodies and invites us into the practice of solitude and secrecy. These are disciplines of withdrawal and disconnection, a way of making space for a truly intimate, personal relationship with God.

I've come to wonder whether these aren't the key disciplines for living the Christian life today. They are almost certainly the starting place. Some might find that thought odd. Why not prayer? Why not Scripture reading or Scripture meditation? The reason is, we need to cultivate and protect that "darker ground" in which our faith can be nourished and nurtured. We need to break the habits of display and discover what it means to be alone with God. Otherwise, the disciplines become just one more way of performing for a crowd.

In 1975, Hannah Arendt received the Sonning prize—an award given in Denmark for contributions to European culture. Arendt felt a certain discomfort with the honor, and part of that stemmed from the resistance she felt about being a public figure. In her acceptance speech, she acknowledged this, describing this public role as a "persona":

> [The word] *persona*, at any event, originally referred to the actor's mask that covered his individual "personal" face and indicated to the spectator the role and the part of the actor in the play. But in this mask, which was designed and determined by the play, there existed a broad opening at the place of the mouth through which the individual, undisguised voice of the actor could sound. It is from this sounding through that the word *persona* was derived: per-sonare, "to

sound through," is the verb of which *persona*, the mask, is the noun.[4]

Arendt strongly believed that Shakespeare was right when he said that "all the world's a stage, and all the men and women merely players." We appear and perform in the world, presenting ourselves as this or that. But Arendt knew the danger of confusing these appearances and personas with our real identity. She was willing to appear, for a moment, as a public figure, so long as she and the audience understood that it was a mask she was going to wear and "sound through" for a brief time—after which she would withdraw again to her ordinary, private life.

> When the events for which the mask was designed are over, and I have finished using and abusing my individual right to sound through the mask, things will again snap back into place. Then I, greatly honored and deeply thankful for this moment, shall be free not only to exchange the roles and masks that the great play of the world may offer, but free even to move through that play in my naked "thisness," identifiable, I hope, but not definable and not seduced by the great temptation of recognition which, in no matter what form, can only recognize us as such and such, that is, as something which we fundamentally are not.[5]

The phrase that is so striking to me is "my naked 'thisness,' identifiable . . . but not definable." What Arendt understands is that my appearance in the world, the displayed version of me, is always a reduction of the real me, which is something that cannot be reduced. We "fundamentally are not" the personas we wear, the displayed versions of ourselves. We are far more complex. As C. S. Lewis once put it, if we truly saw a human being for what they are, we either would be tempted to worship or to recoil in horror.[6]

Arendt's comments are helpful in pointing out that the great danger for our souls is not that we show up and "perform" our way through parenting, work, pastoring, teaching, or making art. In fact, doing those things well demands a certain kind of performance. We wear the persona and play the role to the best of our ability. It's our responsibility not to always display the real me in our frailty and brokenness. Attempts to do so are often gross, obnoxious displays of self-deprecation, self-revelation, and false humility. They're rooted in a desire to control people's opinions about us, or even to manipulate them. Instead, we should never be fooled that the persona is the real thing, or the whole thing.

In recent years, I've seen too many of my friends who are pastors fail to do this. In our age of display, they threw themselves whole-hog into the creation of a persona and devoted all of their energy (and often, the energy of several staff members) into the maintenance of the mask they wore. This left the rest of their life and the rest of their soul unattended, and the darkness they ignored or avoided or pretended didn't exist eventually shipwrecked their lives, their careers, and in many cases, their families. This is just as great a temptation for people who aren't in vocational ministry and has equally catastrophic results.

The personas we wear are always more heroic than the real me, and when that becomes the only way we see ourselves, it's fig leaves. It's an attempt to make ourselves redeemed and acceptable, and it will fail every time.

We are not merely whatever role we may play in the world, be it public figure, celebrity, mother, father, engineer, or vending machine repairman. We cannot be reduced so narrowly and trivially. The truest and most real version of us exists primarily and most wholly in the "hidden ground" of solitude. The "temptation of recognition" would draw us out of that hidden ground and seduce us into thinking that the mask—the persona—is the *real* me. And we must resist that temptation with ferocity.

Life often demands that we appear on the stage of the world. Like a mob of kids in the streets, it mocks and shouts and demands we perform. Sometimes we must perform. And sometimes, that performance gets us rewards. People think we're great, and we want them to think we're great. Soon, we believe we're great.

In solitude, that artifice shatters. The real, confusing me shows up, and I have to reckon with it in its mysterious and contradictory wholeness.

John Calvin opens his great theological work *The Institutes of the Christian Religion* by saying that there is no knowledge of God without knowledge of self. In knowing ourselves, in laying down the artifice and pretense that life in the world both invites and imposes, we see the depths of our need for grace. But we can also find a God who knows it entirely, loves us entirely, and invites us to rest.

PATHWAY 4
WITHDRAWING WITH GOD

Most of us are unprepared, spiritually speaking, for what happens in solitude. It may sound strange, but we need to learn to be alone much like we need to learn anything—speaking a language, playing an instrument, or learning a skill. We need to *practice* solitude so that our hearts and minds can fully engage in it and experience the presence of God. With this in mind, there are three ways to make solitude an integrated habit: regular solitude, little solitudes, and extended solitude.

REGULAR SOLITUDE

Regular is a word that needs some redemption in our modern usage. We're so used to superlatives that we tend to be dismissive and suspect of the ordinary. We don't want regular; we want super-sized awesomeness.

But *regular* is a good word, and it's important to embrace it in two senses here. Regular means ordinary. But regular also refers to time. We need solitude to be regular in the sense that it's repeated—a rhythm we return to as Jesus did.

The main challenge of the discipline of solitude is making the time for it. It's no coincidence that Jesus—and innumerable saints after him—woke early to withdraw and pray. We can be alone with God while the world sleeps. Start by setting aside a small window of time, perhaps fifteen to thirty minutes. If necessary, communicate with your family that you need to be alone. If you have an office with some privacy, you might consider showing up for work a little early and using that space for solitude.

I try to wake at 5:00 or 5:30 every day for this practice (though starting that early is far from necessary). I have a nine-year-old who also wakes at the crack of dawn, and getting up before her is challenging. But I like that she sees me keeping the habit. I always stop by and say hello to her and remind her of the habit I'm keeping as she begins her own morning routine. I count it as a bonus that she sees me making this a priority in my life.

A routine is good. Pick a place and stick with it. Bring a cup of coffee or tea with you. Turn off your phone, and if this isn't obvious, turn off all the other noisemakers too—laptops, TVs, computers, tablets, and so on. Regular solitude is where you'll be practicing other disciplines, practices related to word and prayer, or journaling. I'll have more to say about them in the pages to come. For now, let me encourage you to begin this practice with a few moments of intentional silence.

PRACTICING SILENCE

Spend the first few moments calming your body down. It's important to acknowledge that you are entering silence and that this time matters.

Practicing a moment of silence is both very simple and very difficult. The pull of distraction is strong. Rather than fight it, begin by paying attention to it. What thoughts are emerging? What is tugging at you, trying to pull you away from your seat? What are you worried about, or feeling you need to attend to? Rather than thinking of these things as distractions and problems, simply allow them to pass before you, and offer them up to God.

"Lord, I'm really anxious about work today."

"Lord, I want to check my email."

"Father, I feel very unsettled."

Let them pass, and return to listening and noticing as thoughts cross your mind. Ask yourself, what might God be saying to me, here and now? How might he reply to my anxious, busy thoughts?

The goal of this practice is both to be aware of what's happening inside of us and to be attentive to God's presence. By gaining some self-awareness, we know better how to pray, what to journal about, or how to engage with whatever else we might read.

LITTLE SOLITUDES

Throughout the day, we often find ourselves waiting. We wait for our kids to get out of school. We wait on a bus or a subway or in the back of a cab. We wait for appointments at work, or for doctors, or for a kettle to boil or coffee to brew. Most of us have learned to occupy this time with little entertainments. We play Candy Crush or scroll through Facebook, Instagram, or Twitter, or we read the news or flip through magazines. And while there's nothing wrong with any of these things, I want to propose that we intentionally seize some of those opportunities as little solitudes—invitations to acknowledge that God is present, that he cares about you, and that he is at work.

Breath prayers can be a great tool. As you sit, take a deep breath and say to yourself, "Come, Lord Jesus," or "In him I live, move, and have my being." It's easy to imagine how just that prayer can transform the way you see yourself and your circumstances. If you find yourself struggling to be loving and compassionate, a prayer like "Lord, help me love my neighbors" can similarly transform your experience. If you're anxious on your way to a meeting, let that thought pass before God.

These little solitudes, you'll discover, can fill your days. There are many, many opportunities to be reminded that we live in a world that is rich with God's presence. Closing your eyes and breathing a short prayer may seem like it's nothing at all, but that's disenchantment talking. Practiced regularly, you'll discover an interior silence even in the midst of daily busyness and chaos. It's precisely in these seemingly insignificant moments that we can experience God's transforming presence.

EXTENDED SOLITUDES

Extended solitudes are longer periods of time—a full day or even a few days—where we withdraw from daily life to be alone with God. It can be enormously difficult to make such a retreat happen, especially when time off work can be scarce and the demands of a busy family can be immense. Nonetheless, I encourage you to seek it out. Little can replace the value of an extended time in solitude spent praying, reflecting, and listening to God.

Solitude isn't an end in itself. It's rather like one half of a breath. It's the inhale, and life in community, life among our family, neighbors, coworkers, and friends, is the exhale. It's meant to prepare us for all of life by rooting us firmly in the hiddenness that is ours in Christ, the covering of God's mercy.

The world is a hostile place. We retreat into solitude not out of fear but out of sober preparation for life in a fallen, disenchanted world. We retreat and find what we're so tempted to look for everywhere else.

FIVE

Abundance
and Scarcity

My great aunt Jenny was a character straight out of a Rick Bragg story. A classic southern woman. She lived in a house by a creek in Miami, a pale green atomic ranch with lime green doors and shutters. Everything around the house was green, too—the live oaks, the banyan trees, the algae and lily pads floating at the edge of the creek. We visited often when I was a kid. She spoke slowly with a drawl she brought to Florida from Alabama, and every family gathering involved some discussion of her key lime pie.

She had deep faith and deep wisdom that she passed on via aphorisms that my dad calls "Aunt Jennyisms." "There are no coincidences," she would say, "and there are no secrets." She warned that "nothing good happens after midnight" and that "you can't relive yesterday" and told us to "never worry about anything that a dollar can fix."

These comments hint, for good or ill, at a world that is bigger and more mysterious than we can see. A world where actions have consequences, where our souls are vulnerable but also a world where something mysterious might just be at work for good. A world that remains enchanted.

I think of fairy tales as relics. They come to us from an age when humanity had yet to assume mastery of all things, and they pass along an understanding of how the world works. Like Aunt Jenny's world, fairy tales promise that evil has consequences, that there are no coincidences, and that there is a path of goodness through the world.

In our disenchantment we dismiss these stories as if the story-tellers were superstitious or even stupid. We know better. We know that there are no fairies, no princesses in high castles, no dragons lurking within the hearts of evil people. But we're missing the point: the point of a fairy tale isn't to say that this or that *happened*. I'm sure that many who heard them remained skeptical about the presence of fairies in the woods. But I'm also sure that these stories shaped and reflected their sense of how life works.

One of my favorites is a story I discovered in Lewis Hyde's *The Gift*.[1] It's a strange Scottish folk tale called "The Girl and the Dead Man." It's about a mother who sends her three daughters out into the world. As each is about to leave, their mother offers a choice: they may take a small loaf of bread and a blessing or a large loaf and a curse.

The first daughter chooses the large loaf and the curse and goes on her way. She encounters birds who ask her to share her bread. She refuses. The birds' mother repeats the curse of the girl's mother, and so she is left to eat alone. Night comes and though she has eaten, she's still hungry. She sleeps poorly, cold, in the wild. The next day, she's hired to watch over the dead brother of an old woman because his restless body gets up during the night. She takes the job, but, tired and hungry, falls asleep. The woman kills her for failing at her duty. The second daughter's story is exactly like the first, and both daughters' corpses end up in a pile of trash behind the old woman's house.

The youngest daughter chooses the small loaf and the blessing. She too meets the birds, but she shares her bread, and though the loaf was smaller, all of them eat and are full. In gratitude, the birds wrap her in their wings, keeping her warm so that she sleeps through the night. The next day, when she's hired to watch over the dead man, she's able to stay alert to whack him with a stick when he sits up. As a result, she not only earns her wages but is also given a magic cordial, which she pours on the bodies of her sisters, resurrecting them.

Hyde says the difference between the older daughters and the younger is in how they treat their mother's gift. For the older sisters, what's at stake is the bread itself—something they can see and taste and carry in their sacks. The bread is a commodity to be accumulated and protected. So of course they can't share their bread with the birds. What guarantee is there that another meal is imminent?

The younger daughter knows that something more than bread is at stake. It's a gift—something that wasn't hers to begin with—and meant to be shared.

Another way to describe the difference between the older daughters and the younger is that the younger knew the world was *enchanted*. The older daughters invited the curse upon themselves, thinking, "What harm could a curse do to me?" To them, the bread was real; the curse was superstition. And, of course, they found they were hungry at the end of the day. Maybe, as someone else once said, we do not live on bread alone.

The younger daughter lived in a different world. A blessing was more important to her than the bread. Sharing the gift was more important than protecting it. In turn, the world revealed itself to be abundant—providing her with all she needed and more.

Throughout *The Gift*, Lewis Hyde explores the difference between gifts (given freely, out of a sense of excess and love) and commodities (measured by their exchange value). More broadly, he reveals the difference between an attitude of abundance and an attitude of scarcity.

Commodities work on all the principles of economics and exchange that you might have learned in high school. If you wanted to make and sell electric nose-hair trimmers, you would try to find a customer base that wanted to buy them. The value of your electric nose-hair trimmers would be based on some calculus involving the cost of making them and the market's enthusiasm to buy them.

A gift is entirely different. A gift's value is in the way it makes and reaffirms bonds between people. It's an expression of a relationship. This isn't to say that the cost of a gift doesn't matter, but it certainly isn't the most important thing about the gift. When I give you a gift, I'm not just giving you a gift; I'm giving you something of myself.

The silly gifts our kids give us when they're young mean the world to us because we know that it's not the thing itself that matters, and not even the thought that counts, but the affirmation, unspoken but fundamental to every gift, that you matter to the child, that the bond between us is intact and secure.

Gifts often inspire gifts in return, and many relationships have cycles of gift giving. This can be a good thing so long as there's no sense of obligation and no sense that one person is giving in order to get something in return. If that spirit creeps into the exchange of gifts, then gift giving loses its meaning. This happens at Christmastime— when gift giving can feel forced and joyless. It can also happen in social situations where gift giving can be a way of trying to climb a social ladder or to affirm a hierarchy.

For some of us, Christmas becomes so full of these obligation exchanges that we loathe the season. What's interesting is that in the midst of a season like that, a real gift—a real act of generosity from someone who loves you—can still happen, still break through the callouses we've built up while trying to survive the Christmas season, and touch us deeply.

The other way to destroy the relational bonds of gift giving is to turn a gift into a commodity. Let's say it's my birthday. Ten friends come over to my house, and we eat a good meal, and they all bring a thoughtful gift—books I've wanted or food or what-have-you. So I open my presents and I'm very happy. At the end of the night, just before they leave the house, one friend asks, "What did you think? Good birthday celebration?"

I lean back, survey the gifts that are spread across the table, and say, "Yeah, pretty good. I figure I can get about 350 bucks for all this stuff on eBay after you leave."

If my friend believed I was serious—and more importantly, if I *were* serious—I would have harmed our relationship. In these gifts, my friends weren't just giving me a book or a good record; they were giving me a little something of themselves. Whatever you want to call that extra something that is given with a gift, it's destroyed when I exchange the gifts on the market. It disappears.

At the same time, receiving a gift involves valuing the gift itself. You can imagine a particularly saccharine kid of eight or nine, who at their birthday party opens each gift and thanks each giver by disinterestedly tossing the gift aside and shouting, "But what I really love is *YOU*," bear-hugging each giver, over and over. This would be cute once or twice, but eventually I'd get a stress headache. It would feel insincere, and the child would be missing the point. Honoring the gift is an important part of honoring the giver.

A gift is a whole that is greater than the sum of its parts. Gifts are an expression of love and affection, but they're a little bit more than just that. They're a material good of some kind, but they're more than that too. I'm certain there are psychological and sociological arguments that can account for this "something more" in a disenchanted, materialist way, but I'm not inclined to believe them. I think gifts reveal something about the soulfulness of the world and are an ordinary way we find ourselves trafficking in realities that are mostly unseen.

The Gift goes on to argue that creativity functions best when it's treated like a gift. Artists who do the very best work, he says, recognize themselves as somehow "gifted" and, through their life and work, somehow multiply that gift by giving the world their art. Once art becomes about exchange values—what kind of money or fame or power we might get out of it—we somehow destroy the gift, and it becomes less than what we began with. Trying to exploit our gifts, hoard them, or drain every nickel out of them seems to dry them up.

This is why people talk about artists "selling out." When art becomes a commodity, it loses part of the quality that makes it compelling to its audience. People grow disillusioned with artists, musicians, and actors who seem interested only in making money. This isn't to say that artists shouldn't be paid for their work but rather that getting paid shouldn't be the primary motivation of an artist. Instead, the primary work of an artist is to nurture their gift and multiply it, to give something new to the world. There's a place for patronage and a place for selling art, but the artist must carefully guard the fence that separates the economics of their life and the process of making the art itself.

This too might be explainable in materialist terms, but I can't imagine that those arguments are compelling. Creativity, like gifts, also seems to be an ordinary way that we traffic in the soulfulness of the world.

⁓

The difference between life in a Cosmos and life in a universe is the difference between a gift and a commodity. If the world is a commodity, then like the older sisters in "The Girl and the Dead Man," we should hoard for ourselves as much as we can.

But if we live in a Cosmos—an ordered, meaningful world—then all we have is a gift, and we're invited to respond accordingly. In a lecture, Lewis Hyde once summed up the message of his book as "gratitude that leads to generosity." This could not only summarize a Christian vision for generosity—a grateful creation responding to all they have with open hands—but for the existence of the Cosmos itself. It's a window into the heart of God.

In *The Divine Conspiracy,* Dallas Willard describes watching surf break upon a shoreline.

> **If we live in a Cosmos —an ordered, meaningful world— then all we have is a gift.**

It is perhaps strange to say, but suddenly I was extremely happy for God, and thought I had some sense of what an infinitely joyous consciousness he is and of what it might have meant for him to look at his creation and find it "very good."... He is simply one great inexhaustible and eternal experience of all that is good and true and beautiful and right.[2]

It's easy to imagine a God who calls creation "good" and who delights in the goodness of creation, but we shouldn't stop there. The goodness of creation is itself a product of the goodness of the mind of God. If creativity is gratitude that leads to generosity, then creation might just be the result of God's gratitude for God—an idea that only makes sense if God is three in one. It's God's selfless love for God—or more specifically, the exchange of love and adoration that happens between Father, Son, and Holy Spirit—that leads to gratitude, and that gratitude then leads to the ultimate gesture of generosity: not just creation but the whole redemptive storyline of creation, fall, redemption, and restoration. It's a joyful and grateful God delighting in his own character and goodness who overflows with gratitude and calls everything into existence.

The church fathers called this interchange between the members of the Trinity *perichoresis*, which suggests something like "sacred dance" and implies the glory-sharing movement from member to member of the Trinity, seen in glimpses throughout the Scriptures: Jesus describing how good the work of the Spirit will be when he's sent, the Father glorifying the Son at his Baptism, the Spirit glorifying the Father and the Son in the book of Acts.

It's the nature of the person of God to defer to the other—the Father to the Son, the Son to the Father, the Spirit to the Father and the Son. Each member of the Trinity is enamored with the others, and their love swells them with gratitude. The Cosmos is the ultimate gift from which all others are born.

Throughout the Bible, we can see how gifting and generosity shape the way God interacts with humanity and the life to which he calls them. Paul's phrase, quoting Jesus—"It's more blessed to give than to receive"—is shorthand for much about the character of God and the nature of the Cosmos. It sums up the whole economy of the gospel and the life of Jesus.

Jesus told the woman at the well, "If you knew the gift of God, and who it is that is saying to you, 'Give me a drink,' you would have asked him, and he would have given you living water" (Jn 4:10).

Paul explicitly described gospel as a gift: "But the free gift is not like the trespass. For if many died through one man's trespass, much more have the grace of God and the free gift by the grace of that one man Jesus Christ abounded for many" (Rom 5:15) and "For by grace you have been saved through faith. And this is not your own doing; it is the gift of God" (Eph 2:8).

God's grace is given as a gift, and the way that gift functions is much as Hyde describes the nature of gifts. It flows from God's abundance, it bears fruit in God's people, and it multiplies in the expansion of God's church and God's kingdom.

If the gospel is a gift economy writ large in the Bible, we see it in the minutia as well. We see it in the way people responded to Jesus. Healing is a gift, and those who receive it overflow with praise. Some rush to the temple to praise God. Some follow Jesus. Lives are changed. Elsewhere, social outcasts are given grace and welcomed into the kingdom of God. The woman at the well receives this gift in John 4 and draws the whole town to Jesus. Gratitude leads to generosity. It leads people to share and celebrate what Jesus has done, which draws more people to Jesus.

Another example is the widow and her mite:

> Jesus looked up and saw the rich putting their gifts into the offering box, and he saw a poor widow put in two small copper coins. And he said, "Truly, I tell you, this poor widow has put in more than all of them. For they all contributed out

of their abundance, but she out of her poverty put in all she had to live on." (Lk 21:1-4)

This story, too, underlines the principles of the gift. The widow gives like the youngest daughter in "The Girl and the Dead Man"— with a spirit of abundance. She can give all she has because she has a confidence that there's more to the world than what she can see or what she can possess.

When Jesus feeds the five thousand, we see the power of the gift as well. Jesus tells the disciples to feed the crowd, but all they have are a few loaves and fish. The initial response of the disciples is one of fear and scarcity. Andrew asks, "What are they for so many?" But Jesus gives thanks and distributes the food. There is gratitude, there is generosity, and there is abundance—enough to fill twelve baskets with leftovers.

Yet another example is from Exodus 20, where God sends manna to feed Israel in the wilderness. This passage is an overt demonstration of how the nature of God's provision is a gift, not an exchange. No matter how they gathered, no one had any left over and no one lacked what they needed; each one had just enough. And if anyone tried to keep extra—turning the gift into a commodity to be accumulated and perhaps exchanged—it rotted and became worm infested.

Lewis Hyde cites a fairy tale that mirrors this. In Wales, there were stories about fairies who gave bread to the poor. If they didn't eat the bread on the same day, it turned to toadstools.[3] One doesn't need to believe in fairies to know that something true is revealed by the story.

Contrast this with the alternative of life in a universe, a place where there are no promises for provision at all, where resources are scarce, and where it's up to us to make sure we have what we need. There is an echo of the serpent in Eden in this way of seeing the world: "Has God given you *nothing* to eat?" And there is an echo of Eve in our disenchanted response. We grasp and we hoard and, most deeply, we hope that what we find can make us feel whole.

A few years ago, James K. A. Smith described a trip to the mall in the language of pilgrimage, with a shopper moving through the timeless, seasonless cathedral, looking at displays of "the good life" that hang in store windows.[4] David Foster Wallace made a similar observation in *The Pale King*, calling the shopping mall the "modern functional analog of medieval cathedrals (with some of the parallels downright striking)."[5]

Less than a decade has passed since Smith and Wallace made these observations, and they're a bit dated already. Today, more and more of our shopping is online. We shop as disembodied individuals, never having to encounter another human being. And yet the motivations of shopping remain. We are, like all pilgrims before us, still on a quest for the good life, for something transcendent. That longing combines with our temptation to grasp and hoard and with a sense of the world's scarcity, and consumerism is born.

> While gratitude and abundance are the heart of generosity, dissatisfaction is the fuel of our consumer culture, provoking our longings and directing them at products.

While gratitude and abundance are the heart of generosity, dissatisfaction is the fuel of our consumer culture, provoking our longings and directing them at products. The sense that something is missing from our lives—the sense of scarcity that pervades a godless, disenchanted world—is answered by ads for products that say, "I have what you've been looking for."

A recent Ford commercial showed a truck with four friends inside, hauling dirt bikes out into the desert. "A man," says the gravel-throated narrator, whose voice has more than a little cowboy swagger, "A man and his truck and some company." Images flash by of the friends unloading the bikes and riding over sand dunes. The narrator talks about hard landings and sore vertebrae and how the three-hour drive home will make it all melt away.

The commercial isn't actually advertising the truck; it's offering a lifestyle, an identity. The truck makes available a way of life: "Here is someone's authentic and rich experience, someone who knows who they are and is living 'the good life.' Imagine yourself there, with real friends and real adventures. Imagine all the scenes that this truck could make available." Rather than meeting our needs for transportation and hauling, it offers to satisfy a deeper longing.

This is why ads use sexually evocative images to sell everything from cheeseburgers to tires. They aren't trying to rationally convince us; they're simply trying to stir desire and connect it to whatever they're selling.

My favorite example of the way consumer products offer a sense of identity is wearable activism. The RED campaign sells products many would buy already—Gap, Nike, and Apple products, for example—and gives a portion of the proceeds to relief work around the world. By branding them with the RED campaign, the consumer gets to feel altruistic. They also get the added benefit of being able to display their altruism. Tom's Shoes has thrived on the same model, making the center of their ad campaigns the fact that for each pair of shoes purchased, one is given away. These products activate a disenchanted trifecta in our hearts: a desire to feel good about ourselves, a product to buy/hoard in a scarce world, and the chance to display our goodness to others.

Philosopher and cultural critic Slavoj Žižek is a brutal critic of this sort of thing. In a lecture, he talked about how Starbucks made a big deal about donating a tiny fraction of their overpriced coffee to "some stupid Guatemala children or whatever."[6] If you think that sounds harsh and dismissive, that is Žižek's exact point: people like that Starbucks donates this money because of how it makes them feel about themselves, not because of deep concern for the actual children. We hardly think of the children . . . until Žižek calls them stupid.

Similarly, there's a massive market for consumer goods that display our faith. Like wearable activism, buying a Christian t-shirt or bumper sticker feels like we're doing something for our faith. From the marketing side, people make a great deal of money selling everything from books to retreats, preying on the hope that the product will satisfy our spiritual longings.

More broadly Žižek suggests that we're never being sold products themselves; we're always being sold something more, something that taps into our longing for the transcendent. Coca-Cola is one of the foremost examples of this when they sell us sugary fizzy-water and say, "Coke is it!" or "It's the real thing." In his trademark style, Žižek asks, "What is it, 'The Real Thing'? It's not just another positive property of Coke, something that can be described and pinpointed through chemical analysis, it's that mysterious something more. The undescribable excess which is the cause of my objective desire."[7]

Coke doesn't say, "Drink and be refreshed."[8] Instead, it projects a deeper meaning. It's "The Real Thing"—an experience we long for.

And the ads work. I don't consciously assent to the idea that a new razor is going to make me irresistible to women, but the ad's power isn't necessarily conscious. I don't have to believe it to be true; I only have to wish it were true.

When we find ourselves in a wilderness drained of any connection to God or transcendence, we nonetheless search for a sense of meaning and identity. We can't root it in anything with depth, but we can root it in something shallow—what we wear, what we drive, what we eat.

The opportunities present themselves and we pounce, handing over cash and swiping our cards in grasping attempts to satisfy our hungry hearts. The market cheers us on and the debts rack up, and yet satisfaction seems as scarce and short-lived as ever.

Whatever we might display through our consumption, whatever identity we take on, it fails to transform us. Change of the heart is *hard*, and so we settle for the veneer. This, too, reveals our disenchantment. If we really believed God's kingdom was here, why would we keep doing things the same way? Why would we settle for so little?

To quote Tyler Durden again, "The things you own end up owning you. It's only after you lose everything that you're free to do anything." There's a remarkable biblical resonance with this line. Our grasping to own, to consume, to possess—all of it only ends up binding us further. Consumerism only makes sense if the world is a place where resources are scarce, where God can't be counted on to show up or provide for us. We need to hoard what we have, grab what we can, and keep as much for ourselves as possible.

But that approach always fails. It bumps its head up against the hard stone of reality. Moths and bugs eat away at stored grain. Housing prices plummet. Interest rates go up. Commissions go down. Stored manna turns to rot. Hoarded bread turns to toadstools. However much we have, there is always something more we could have that's just out of reach. The harder we grasp, the less the bread satisfies, the colder the night gets, and the wearier our souls feel.

The world doesn't work when we approach it this way. At the heart and helm of all of creation is a God of abundance. The Psalms describe his Word as a lamp unto our feet and a light unto our path, lighting the steps ahead of us. He offers us his presence in the here-and-now, not at some faraway destination. He provides

> At the heart and helm of all of creation is a God of abundance.

what we need for *this* day, and there are new mercies *this* morning. Life in the Cosmos is a life of abundance and a life of dependence, a life of daily bread and fresh manna.

We can only hold loosely what we know was not ours to begin with. In an abundant world, all we have is a gift, and a gift inspires joy and generosity. Our lives are not about possession but provision, not about what we consume but what we've been given and thus what we can share.

PATHWAY 5
PRACTICING ABUNDANCE

Part of what separates a spirit of abundance and a spirit of scarcity is a sense of deep-rooted satisfaction. Dissatisfaction (as I have already noted) is the fuel of consumerism, and coupled with fear and anxiety, it drives us to all kinds of frenetic spending, grabbing, and hoarding.

In a scarce world, we always grasp for more, and we find ourselves ever more deeply unhappy. But in a world of abundance, we find satisfaction in places that don't depend on what we possess or what we consume.

There are two practices that I believe help train us to live with a spirit of abundance: fasting and generosity.

FASTING

As I write this, it's Ash Wednesday, the first day of the forty-day Lenten fast in anticipation of Easter. Traditionally, Christians fast by eating only two small meals and one "normal" meal per day, with no meat on Fridays or Saturdays until Easter. These days, some mark it by giving up chocolate, desserts, or sugar, but most folks don't mark it at all.

Fasting, like any practice, can be meaningless if we undertake it seeking religious self-improvement. That said, I've never—not once—in sixteen years of pastoring had to confront or challenge someone whose fasting was too public or too self-righteous. The practice has all but disappeared from many Christian traditions.

There are several related reasons for this.

The first is cultural changes within the church. Liberalism, fundamentalism, and evangelicalism have each done their part in disconnecting Christianity from the church's traditions and the church year. When you lose Advent and Lent, you lose the practices that come with them: seasons of lament, mourning, and fasting.

Along with this culture shift come two others. The first is a shift toward knowledge as the pathway to discipleship. The emphasis is on what's in our heads, and the idea of training our bodies seems unnecessary (or more likely, goes unconsidered at all).

Finally, I think fasting disappears because we're disenchanted. If there's nothing beyond what we might see, touch, taste, and feel, then a fast, a season like Lent, or a day like Ash Wednesday makes no sense. What could we possibly expect to happen on the other side of a fast except for discomfort and hunger?

Together, these reasons combine to making fasting a largely unpracticed thing, even by people who've studied it significantly. This is my story—I read about fasting for *years* before integrating it as a practice in my life, and I still feel as if I barely understand how to make it meaningful. But I show up for the fasts—the annual fasts and more personal, shorter fasts—in confidence that practice will make the experience richer over time.

Fasting only makes sense in a world where, to borrow a phrase, "man does not live on bread alone." It only makes sense when there might be something transcendent possible, some opportunity on the other side of hunger, some deeper satisfaction, some food that the world of the visible knows nothing about.

It also only makes sense in the midst of a life where we know how to feast—how to attend, with gratitude and joy, to a meal that comes as a gift.

But fasting comes first in a fallen world. In fasting, we turn to those who are suffering. We turn to our own poverty and our rampant appetites. We attend to brokenness, not to solve it or understand it but merely to behold it and cry, "Come, Lord Jesus."

Put it into practice. Like anything in the Christian life, fasting is an invitation, not an obligation, and we need to learn to walk in it before we can run. So don't be a hero, and don't do something stupid like going many days without food or water for your first fast.

Start simple. For fasting to become a habit, it must be done regularly. So to start, I'd encourage you to pick one day a week in which you'll practice fasting. On that day, you'll skip normal meals for breakfast and lunch, and eat again at dinner time. For your first three to four weeks, don't go entirely without food for these fasts—just shrink your meals down to something light and simple: a piece of fruit and a granola bar, or a smoothie, or just a glass of juice. In the time that you'd normally spend eating that meal, make time to pray. Read Scripture or other spiritual writing, or write in a journal. I'll often go for a walk and pray.

Pick a focus. Having something specific to pray for helps focus a fast—when you have hunger pangs or you arrive at set-aside times to pray, you don't have to think about what you're praying for. So pick something specific, and the more specific the better. Don't just pray for "poverty," pray for some specific poor people or for a ministry that is serving the poor. Don't just pray for "the church," pray for your church—praying for people by name or focusing your prayers on a specific pastor or two. Making a choice like this can be difficult because we always have too many people to pray for, but remember that you're cultivating a habit. If you do this once a week, you can pray intently for fifty-two people, ministries, or needs a year.

Stretch. Once you've made a particular day of the week a fast day, and your body has begun to adjust to going for a longer period with less food, you can begin to stretch. There are two ways to do this. One is to go with less food in that window—shrinking down to just water or just liquids—or to extend the time, skipping more meals. If you extend time, I'd encourage you to do that no more than once a month or so. You might try stretching in both directions over time to see how your mind and body react and what feels like the best way to intensify your focus on prayer.

Plan and be responsive. The church calendar is a great resource for thinking about fasting as a rhythm of life. There are longer seasons of fasting, like Advent and Lent, and there are specific fast days. I always find it helpful to think about the church calendar as the work of pastors who tried to shape the lives of Christians around the story of the gospel. Fasting and feasting, in regular rhythms, call us to the sorrows of the world that awaits redemption and the foretaste of redemption that we have now in Jesus Christ.

So with that in mind, however you might structure it, some regularity in fasting is a good thing. Likewise, be responsive to your life. When a trial arises in your life or in the life of someone near to you, or when you arrive at a crossroads with a difficult decision before you, enter a fast, focus your prayers, and draw near to God.

GENEROSITY

The second practice that roots us in a world of abundance is generosity. By giving away our money, we learn that what we have is a gift to begin with. I don't believe there's any other pathway to learning that it's more blessed to give than receive.

In 2 Corinthians 8–9, Paul writes about the generosity of the Macedonian Christians. At the time, they were "severely afflicted," suffering persecution from a hostile community around them. And yet their suffering and poverty led them to overflow with a "wealth of generosity." It's a story that only makes sense in an abundant world.

Paul paints a picture of generosity that's driven not by guilt or compulsion but joy. Those who give quite literally have a fear of missing out. The Macedonians actually begged the apostles to let them give—a situation that I've never seen in sixteen years of ministry.

Putting it into practice. I find it helpful to think of generosity in three categories: gospel ministry, mercy, and hospitality.

Gospel ministry refers to the work of the church, and especially refers to our covenant communities—the congregations where we gather. We ought to make it a priority to support the work of those who are looking after our souls. As I said in chapter five, gratitude leads to generosity. We might struggle to be generous to our churches because we lack a grateful spirit for what that community means for us.

Mercy is a broad term that invites us to consider those around us in need: giving to the poor, to fight human trafficking, to a friend whose car broke down, to a neighbor who needs a new lawn mower, or to a family member swamped with medical bills.

Hospitality refers to the habit of welcoming people into our lives and our dinner tables. Doing so requires a spirit of abundance and a willingness to break out the good ice cream and extra helpings of food.

All of these habits require planning, but most of all they require a heart rooted in the joy of the gospel and a confidence that we do not live by bread alone. As my Aunt Jenny said, never worry about anything that a dollar can fix, and as Paul told the Corinthians, to miss out on giving is to miss out on joy. Knowing that we live in an abundant world with a generous God can free us to do both.

SIX

Feasts of Attention

Much ink has been spilled over shrinking attention spans in the age of the smartphone. I've spilled some of that ink myself. But I'm not sure it's fair to blame the problem entirely on technology. Perhaps attention spans have grown short because a disenchanted world fails to give much reason to attend to anything at all. If the background of our lives is that the world is empty, meaningless, and destined to be forgotten, it's hard to justify investing ourselves deeply in something—a relationship, a novel, or a even movie—that isn't immediately pleasant or, at the very least, distracting. This, like so many burdens, applies equally to Christians and non-Christians.

David Foster Wallace wrote about this in his novel *The Pale King*, questioning why dullness is

> such a powerful impediment to attention.... Maybe it's be-
> cause dullness is intrinsically painful; maybe that's where
> phrases like "deadly dull"or "excruciatingly dull" come from.
> But there might be more to it. Maybe dullness is associated
> with psychic pain because something that's dull or opaque fails

to provide enough stimulation to distract people from some other, deeper type of pain that is always there, if only in an ambient low-level way, and which most of us spend nearly all our time and energy trying to distract ourselves from feeling, or at least from feeling directly or with our full attention. Admittedly, the whole thing's pretty confusing, and hard to talk about abstractly. . . . But surely something must lie behind not just Muzak in dull or tedious places anymore but now also actual TV in waiting rooms, supermarkets' checkouts, airports' gates, SUV's backseats. Walkmen, iPods, BlackBerries, cell phones that attach to your head. This terror of silence with nothing diverting to do. I can't think anyone really believes that today's so-called "information society" is just about information. Everyone knows it's about something else, way down.[1]

What if the trouble with attention isn't merely that we've been trained for constant stimulation but also that constant stimulation is addictive precisely because it distracts us from the anxieties of disenchantment?

This could account for not only the shortness of our attention spans but also the shallowness of them. Anything that demands a depth of attention—something like a work of art, a novel, or even a substantive conversation with another human being—exposes our humanity and forces us to reckon with what Charles Taylor calls the "malaise" of disenchantment. In a world without transcendence, what we experience in those moments is something akin to bumping your head on a low ceiling. They draw us into the heights and depths of our humanity—the world of art, beauty, music, and darkness, of love and romance and bitterness and sorrow—none of which have a truly satisfactory explanation in a disenchanted world. They confront us with something too big to explain in terms that deny transcendence.

As Charles Taylor describes it, there is something painful to this experience. We feel like we're on the outside looking in at a feast, but our disenchantment blocks the door and we remain in the grey cold.

We can avoid that pain with a thousand distractions, bite-sized entertainments that allow us to float blissfully in the shallow waters of life, each two-minute YouTube clip and 140-character tweet arriving like another wave of distracting energy.

God pays attention. He truly attends to his creation. We celebrate it in dozens of phrases that are almost clichés: His eye is on the sparrow. He owns the cattle on a thousand hills. Every hair on your head is numbered. Before he formed you in the womb, he knew you. Perhaps we could re-label the doctrine of God's providence as the promise that God is paying attention.

It's not enough, though, to point out that God pays attention to these things. As G. K. Chesterton points out in *Orthodoxy*, the sun rises each day because God never tires of saying "Do it again" to the sun. Every daisy looks alike not out of some mechanical necessity, but because God likes the way they look, and likes making them over and over again.[2] God's attention is God's delight. When he pays attention, he invests whatever he is attending to with his immense joy.

And the miracle of God's providence is that he's paying attention to all of it.

Life with God reorders the world and invites us into silence and solitude, where our simmering anxieties and sorrows can be brought into God's healing presence. But it isn't simply a call to withdrawal. We're invited to pay attention to the enchanted world around us in a new way, to be open to the possibility of an encounter with God at every moment. Simone Weil once said that attention, at its most realized, is like prayer.[3] To pay attention

All ground is holy ground.

is to *attend to* something, to be present. We attend because the world isn't cold and empty but filled with presence of God. Every moment, every encounter, is meaningful and numinous. All ground is holy ground.

Robert Capon wrote, "Man's real work is to look at the things of the world and to love them for what they are. That is, after all, what God does, and man was not made in God's image for nothing."[4] For Capon, attention is the paterfamilias of all human innovation and creativity.

> How much curious and loving attention was expended by the first man who looked hard enough at the insides of trees, the entrails of cats, the hind ends of horses, and the juice of pine trees to realize he could turn them all into the first fiddle. No doubt his wife urged him to get up and do something useful.[5]

He wrote this in a book about food called *The Supper of the Lamb* and in a chapter that is entirely devoted to the experience of slicing an onion. He obeys that cardinal rule of writers—"Show, don't tell"—by lovingly attending to that experience. The onion, it turns out, is a window into the mind of God, the wonders of creation, and the goodness of being human. If only we pay it careful enough attention.

> Man's real work is to look at the things of the world and to love them for what they are. That is, after all, what God does, and man was not made in God's image for nothing. The fruits of his attention can be seen in all the arts, crafts, and

sciences. It can cost him time and effort, but it pays handsomely. If an hour can be spent on one onion, think how much regarding it took on the part of that old Russian who looked at onions and church spires long enough to come up with St. Basil's Cathedral.[6]

Commanding attention seems to be the work of artists throughout the ages. In Renaissance sculpture, the artist called us to pay attention to the wonders of the human form and the intricate and delicate work of human faces—each one of which is as unique as a fingerprint or a snowflake. The master painters of that age and their photorealistic creations were a way of calling attention to life, light, the human form, and the drama of the stories they represented.

Later painters such as Monet and Degas and Renoir began to call attention to the way that light plays tricks on us, the way imprecise brushwork could convey a clear impression of whatever object they were attempting to render. Over many decades, the trajectory of visual art leaned more and more toward abstraction—calling attention less to the objects in the art and more to those who are viewing the art, the experience of art, and the experience of seeing. In the last one hundred years, this turn became more radical still—Warhol's paintings of Campbell's soup cans, DuChamp's *Fountain*, Jeff Koons's Hoover vacuums, Damien Hirst's animal carcasses suspended in formaldehyde. In each case, the primary impulse of the artist is the same: they're calling for us to pay attention to something, be it our modern, sterilized society, life in an industrialized world, our obsessive consumerism, or the artifice of the gallery itself.

Encounters with beauty, whether they're in an art gallery, a book, a song, or in the wild, command our attention. They invite us to put away our distractions and our busy thoughts and to be present. We often find it difficult to make room for these things, and I think that in part, it's because they are demanding. We cannot help but be evoked—whether that's toward bliss, sadness, or even rage.

Commanding attention is also the work of those who traffic in food. Wine, cheese, beer, and even bread all have the ability to call our attention to a sense of place—*terroir*—through their flavors. A skillful chef will cook a piece of meat or fish in such a way that we don't taste just any steak or any salmon; we somehow experience the grassiness of the land where the cattle grazed or the briny waters where the salmon lived. It's said that Martin Luther, a great lover of beer, would taste a particularly good brew and exclaim, "Good creature." This is a brilliant act of attention, celebrating gift and giver in a single breath.

To attend to the world simply means to be alive to it and open to possibilities within it. It means to cultivate the awareness that this is a Cosmos—a world that came into existence and continues to exist because of God's words—and that all we encounter and experience is part of a wondrous conversation between us and God. Every moment beckons us to look closer.

Of course, not everything in the Cosmos is a source of unbridled delight. The world is a dark place, full of suffering and death. We inevitably have to face the darkness, no matter how hard we try to distract ourselves from it. It's painful to pay attention to the world.

Job and his friends spend a few lengthy chapters attending to Job's sufferings, trying to sort out why the things that happened happened. They all think that suffering needs answers and that God needs to show up and defend the order of the world—whether it is by defending God's righteousness or Job's. But God shows up and refuses to take part in the debate. He doesn't affirm the world's order; he affirms its mysteriousness.

> Who is this that darkens counsel by words without
>   knowledge?
> Dress for action like a man;
>   I will question you, and you make it known to me.
>   (Job 38:2-3)

In the monologue that follows, God asks a series of questions referencing his work as the Creator: Where were you when I laid the Earth's foundations? What do you know about the origins of the seas? What do you know about creation's heights and depths? He lists out a series of creatures, asking why they run, why they fly, why they're filled with fury and power. It's almost as if he's shouting, "Did you notice this? Did you notice that?"

We are small creatures in a wondrous creation.

It's gorgeous poetry—cascading images of creation—that has two effects on the reader. First, we are filled with wide-eyed wonder at the world that surrounds us, and second, we are reminded how inexplicable that world is. We are small creatures in a wondrous creation.

As G. K. Chesterton describes it, God "comes not to answer riddles, but propound them," insisting to Job (who awaits explanation for his suffering) "that it is a much stranger world than Job ever thought it was":

> God says, in effect, that if there is one fine thing about the world, as far as men are concerned, it is that it cannot be explained. He insists on the inexplicableness of everything. "Hath the rain a father? . . . Out of whose womb came the ice?" (38:28f). He goes farther, and insists on the positive and palpable unreason of things; "Hast thou sent the rain upon the

desert where no man is, and upon the wilderness wherein there is no man?" (38:26) . . . He unrolls before Job a long panorama of created things, the horse, the eagle, the raven, the wild ass, the peacock, the ostrich, the crocodile. He so describes each of them that it sounds like a monster walking in the sun. The whole is a sort of psalm or rhapsody of the sense of wonder. The maker of all things is astonished at the things he has Himself made. . . . Instead of proving to Job that it is an explicable world, He insists that it is a much stranger world than Job ever thought it was.[7]

Slavoj Žižek once summarized Chesterton's commentary on Job by saying that God shows up and says, look around you; the whole world is crazy.[8] As Žižek sees it, Job is a book written to show the pointlessness of meaning-making in the midst of suffering.

My wife and I had a friend who, for many years, any time someone shared a hardship or a story of suffering, would respond by making a strange little clicking sound with her mouth and then say, "Well, I guess God wanted such-and-such to happen." Got a flat tire on the way to pick up your kid at school? "Well, I guess God didn't want you to get there on time." Got rejected from grad school? "Well, I guess God wanted you to use this time for something else." Got cancer? "Well, I guess God wanted you to learn about suffering."

At times it made you wish you had a cold glass of water in your hands to splash in her face.

Comments like this reduce a moment of pain or serious suffering into a quip, a simple lesson from God that "makes sense" of something incredibly frustrating and miserable. There may be a shade of truth in it, but a comment like this fails to account for the whole experience. It fails to account for a God who (to borrow a phrase from the Westminster Catechism) isn't the author of evil. It fails to make sense of a good world gone bad. It serves mostly to comfort the person making the quip; they wrap themselves in feigned understanding of the situation, insulating their own life from the misery of yours.

God doesn't respond to Job's misery with explanations or dismissive comments. Instead, he calls Job's attention to the confusing wonder of the world we live in. He leads Job from the mystery of his suffering to the mysteries of creation, from puzzle to puzzle, from wonder to wonder. And as Chesterton puts it, "The secret of God is a bright and not a sad one."[9] In the skipping of mountain goats, the thunder of snow, and the crashing of oceans, there's a wink and smile, a God who is joyful and even playful in the midst of the madness. While we may not be able to comprehend it, there is—at least to God—sensibility and an order. The universe is a Cosmos after all, and Chesterton tells us its maker has a smile and a sense of humor, even as he reminds us of our smallness in its midst. He calls our attention from the midst of sorrows to the broader world where sorrows are one mystery among many.

Harold Best writes,

> Christians should be as delighted in the things of sight and sense as God is himself, when at the instant of every creational act, he declares goodness to be observable, enjoyable and usable. Of all people, Christians should have the best noses, the best eyes and ears, the most open joy, the widest sense of delight. That the opposite is often the case is no fault of the Lord's. How interesting that God, in correcting the ruminations of Job and his three advisers, turned to his work as Imaginer and Maker rather than to his holiness.[10]

Maybe the secret to reckoning with pain and sorrow isn't meaning-making and answer-seeking but embracing mystery and cultivating wonder. God provides Job with no answers and, somehow, at the end of the book, Job is happy. It turns out he didn't need answers; he needed to be awakened to the beautiful chaos of the Cosmos around him. He needed to embrace the mystery.

I have to admit that I hate myself a little bit for typing the phrase "embrace the mystery." It sounds like either a bad Sarah McLachlan song or the kind of nonsense you'd see plastered on the back of a beat-up Volvo station wagon along with a dozen other pseudospiritual slogans and political statements. And yet, I'll confess to staring at the phrase and thinking about it for a full twenty minutes before moving on. I don't know that there's a better way to put it. We have spent most of our lives hanging our hope on getting answers for the questions in life that perplex and over-whelm us. Our certainty that explanations exist for everything is perhaps the surest sign of our disenchantment. The book of Job, and the Bible in general, seems to shrug all that off. Deuteronomy 29:29 essentially says, "God reveals what he wants to—and be glad for it. But the secrets are all his."

In *Orthodoxy*, Chesterton tells us that the difference between the rationalist and the poet is that the poet seeks to poke his head into the heavens and look around a bit. The rationalist tries to cram the heavens into his head, and more often than not, it's his head that splits.[11] Our clawing, grasping attempts at answering every question and making sense of every mystery in life will end up in failure. Instead, God invites us to take a tour of the mad, mad world around us, to see ourselves as one mystery among the many, and to trust him that it all makes sense in some strange, cosmic way.

In doing so, we discover that the presence of mystery in the world is an invitation to wonder, and a world without mystery is a world of despair. So go ahead; embrace the mystery.

Attention has many enemies. Distraction is an obvious one: we find ourselves content to surf the shallows, not quite present, not quite absent, content instead to be merely entertained. It keeps the real world at arm's length. Cynicism and snobbery likewise help us to keep the world at a safe distance.

Cynicism assumes that everyone is a snake-oil salesman, whether they're selling cars, diet plans, or, well, snake oils. It's not simply skepticism; a skeptic can be optimistic and hopeful as they ask questions.[12] Cynics are pessimistic and often bitter. A cynic believes that everyone's an emperor in "new clothes," arrogantly pretending to know something that simply isn't true. Cynics rob themselves (and others) of joy because they're dismissive of the good that comes from creation, art, and culture; they're convinced that nothing is good, that everything is an empty promise.

David Foster Wallace described cynicism wonderfully in an essay about the way that television had transformed culture in the 1990s. He describes it as a "numb blank bored demeanor—what one friend calls the 'girl-who's-dancing-with-you-but-would-obviously-rather-be-dancing-with-somebody-else' expression." For cynics, everything is kept at a slight remove, as if it were "extant only as performance, awaiting our cool review. . . . Cynicism announces that one knows the score, was last naïve about something at maybe like age four."[13] The cynic won't be fooled by your snake oil, but their posture also prevents them from being wowed by the transcendent or moved by anything beautiful. They live in a cold universe, a world without mystery or wonder.

Snobbery works on the same principle. Snobs might gush about the complex *terroir* of a fifty-dollar bottle of French-oaked Chardonnay and turn their nose up at a ballpark hot dog. They might give long-winded opining lectures on how much they love Bela Bartok and wave off Bruce Springsteen. Where a cynic is suspicious of claims that there's anything transcendent in the world, the snob is suspicious that anything good comes from ordinary, earthy life.

In both cases, the attitude is adopted because we think it protects us from risk. To seek transcendence feels risky, especially in a world where we're already pushing against hard-formed barriers in our hearts and minds. Likewise, enjoying the good of something ordinary pushes against certain disenchanted realities. In a world of mutual display, our "good taste" might be the clearest sign of our religious excellence; we've transcended the common world, and we wouldn't deign to bother with it again.

Both cynicism and snobbery come from an anxious and insecure heart. They are acts of self-protection, ways of insulating ourselves from a world—whether it's high-brow or low-brow—that we feel we're looking at from the outside. The antidote is to pay attention, to be present to the thing we're dismissive of, and, to borrow a biblical phrase, to make our dwelling (literally, to pitch our tents) among those we don't understand. In being present and attentive to that world, we can come to understand it and to see that it, like all of creation, is *good*.

Goodness shows up in the simple and the complex, in Paul McCartney's "Yesterday" and Aaron Copland's "Appalachian Spring," in the complex layers of spice, sweetness, and bitterness that make up a coconut curry and that trinitarian wonder of fat, salt, and sugar—a cheeseburger, fries, and a milkshake.

Attention opens us up to the goodness contained within each of these, and like Capon and the onion, we just might discover that each good thing in turn opens up the Cosmos to the rest of us.

One of the most magical places in the world is the dinner table. It demands our attention in many ways, especially when we share a meal with others. So much culminates at the dinner table—the meal, the relationships of the gathered, and the day itself. In Jewish tradition, the new day is marked by sunset, and dinner has an almost sacramental quality—especially on the Sabbath. It's a time for bonding, for thanksgiving, and for feasting. It's a celebration of all the elements—the food, the people, and the time itself—and a call to pay attention to each one. Every feast is a feast of attention.

Attention differentiates feasting and mere consuming and consumerism. Consuming is about possession, and consuming something uses it up. The end goal of a fast food meal is a pile of empty wrappers. The end goal of most consumer products is obsolescence. We are not meant to dwell with cars, smartphones, and running shoes—not for long, anyway. These things are meant to be used up, and once used up, disposed of or recycled into something new.

The same is true of much of pop culture. Hannah Arendt once pointed out that mass culture doesn't want *culture* in the classic sense—which she defined as art and artifacts that are meant to endure as part of a shared wealth of truth and beauty. Instead, mass culture wants "entertainment, and the wares offered by the entertainment industry are indeed consumed by society just like any other consumer goods." They are "destined to be used up, just like any other consumer goods."[14]

> A feast is about attention, and attention is about presence.

"Planned obsolescence," as it's sometimes called, drives our economy. New iPhones appear, making the previous generation look clumsy and archaic. "The entertainment industry is confronted with gargantuan appetites," Arendt says, "and since its wares disappear in consumption, it must constantly offer new commodities."[15] They capture our attention only long enough for us to consume them, and then they fade.

A feast is different. A feast is about attention, and attention is about presence. To say that a Thanksgiving meal is all about turkey is to miss the point of the feast. But it's not all about the company kept or the time of year either. The feast is made up of all of the elements. At its best, it brings them to a moment in time where they all come together into a soulful, rich experience. Like gifts, feasts are far more than their component parts.

We don't quite know what to do with food these days. Our attitudes toward food run along a spectrum where, at one end, food is one of the only transcendent goods left in the world. From this crowd come foodie culture, pour-over coffee, farm-to-table movements, and artisan chocolate, salt, and bread. At the other end of the spectrum, food is mere fuel, a science to master for the sake of health and longevity.

In the middle come a thousand other attitudes toward food. There are those concerned with the ethics of eating, some of whom advocate for humane and sustainable farming techniques and some of whom are crazy-eyed militant vegans. There are the organic food police who seem to mostly want to critique the foods that parents feed their children, and there are those who believe that paleolithic humans had a monopoly on wisdom and eating. Most folks live the Omnivore's Dilemma (as Michael Pollan called it), driving through McDonald's on the way home from Whole Foods.

When it comes to food, our attention is pulled in a thousand directions: ethical eating, factory farming, proteins, carbs, fats, sugars, artificial sugars—almost anywhere but the Cosmos, wherein food comes as a gift meant to nurture us, to remind us of our dependence on the God who gives it. Feasting only makes sense in a Cosmos, where the good of food comes with a sense of generosity and mystery, and where the table nourishes not only our bodies but also our souls.

In a disenchanted world, there is no Giver, and thus no meaning to food or to the bodies that food sustains. There are only biological functions. Food is just another way of sustaining the temporary animation of the stuff that makes up our lives.

Perhaps the most miserable, soulless, and disenchanted thing in the world is Soylent—a meal-replacement drink that provides "maximum nutrition with minimal effort."[16] It's a smooth, white drink made of bioengineered algae and soy, pumped up with vitamins and minerals to provide "everything the body needs." (This quote is borrowed from *The Matrix*, where it described a hideous, gloopy, oatmeal-like sludge that the humans ate once liberated from their robotic overlords. When it's introduced, one character responds, "It's not *everything* the body needs" as if to say, man doesn't live on bread alone.) Soylent perfectly embodies a world without meaning, a world without soul, where the human body is a machine and food is merely fuel, and where nutrition is a mathematical and chemical problem to solve.

Soylent makes sense only in a world that has been so thoroughly drained of magic and deprived of wonder. It is the foodstuff of a busy society that has too much to do and too many other things to think about and occupy itself with than food or eating. It's the fuel of people on the go, buried in busyness and distraction.

Soylent might be the communion wine of a productivity religion that is too busy to stop working to eat a meal. It might also be the sacrament of a religion that Margaret Somerville called "Healthism"—an obsessive, society-encompassing way of thinking that, like any religion, has its virtues, such as physical fitness, the consumption of "pure" foods, and a preference for vegetables, and vices, such as smoking, watching too much television, and eating fast food.[17] Soylent attempts to perfect life as a mere biological function, sustaining the body with meticulously calculated chemical inputs that minimize the trouble of choice, taste, and time wasted at the table.

Part of me wonders whether Soylent isn't an elaborate prank or the work of a performance artist. Its name has obvious connections to *Soylent Green*, the 1973 film starring Charlton Heston. In that dystopian film, a society suffering from pollution and over-population is fed Soylent Green—a complete nutritional supplement supposedly made from farmed plankton. Heston plays a police detective working a homicide case, and in the process of solving the crime discovers that Soylent Green is actually made from human corpses. The film ends about the time Heston cries out to a crowd, "Soylent Green is made of people!"

While I don't suspect that Soylent is made from people, I do wonder if somewhere someone is laughing quietly to themselves about the fact that they can sell a product that purports to do the same thing and shares the same name. I also wonder if some kind of public punch line is coming—a "Soylent is made of cheeseburgers" moment of some sort. Unfortunately, I think the priests of Healthism behind this product take themselves far too seriously to give us such a wondrous gift.

It's no wonder that of all the metaphors that fill the pages of the Song of Solomon, food and feasting seem to be the dominant theme. Sex is a feast of attention. It is most intimate and most meaningful when a husband and wife approach one another in a spirit of generosity, joy, and wonder. In a broken world, it becomes the collision of two bodies, a mere pleasure exchange that avoids any real spiritual or relational intimacy. At its worst, it becomes something much darker—the stuff of human trafficking and an oppressive sex industry.

Christians don't seem to know what to do with this topic. When I was a kid, the message was essentially, "Sex is filthy, dirty, and disgusting (so save it for the one you love)." And while I'm sure that prudishness and fear-mongering sexual education still abounds, in general, it seems like the pendulum has swung the other way. Now, there are legions of books, pastors, and conferences telling us that sex is (to borrow a phrase from Ferris Bueller) the end-all-be-all of human existence. There are websites that market sex toys to Christians, Christians who blog about the intimate details of their sex lives, and (as I mentioned in an earlier chapter) there is a pastor who wrote a book about sex and then spent twenty-four hours broadcasting with his wife in a bed on the roof of his church to promote it. They were clothed, thank God.

Christians talk about sex as though they're trying to keep up with a world that is using sex to market everything and that markets everything with the promise of better sex. Christians are worried about having sex that's as good or better than the sex they think non-Christians are having. There's a whole Christian Sexual Entertainment Complex running on the fear of missing out, and the only thing that's certain is that Christians *must* be missing out.

So pastors and writers talk about Christian alternatives to the world's way of spicing up the bedroom while offering how-to guides to maximizing our pleasure. A few years ago, a controversial book was published that outlined many of these topics—the use of sex toys, the benefits of video and photography, and the ethics of various sex acts. (I believe just about everything got a green light so long as it involved only two people.) The best response to this book came from Douglas Wilson and could be summarized in the following quote:

> The apostle Paul says nothing about video-recording a marital sex act on your cell phone. This is because he wrote to the Ephesians, to the Galatians, and not to the Idiots. If he were writing to the Idiots, he might have felt constrained to mention it. Oh, no, you might reply, feeling a little stung by my insensitive use of the word Idiot with an upper case I, you and your wife are being "very careful." *Very* careful. I see. So careful that when you both die in a car wreck nobody is going to go through your effects?[18]

The word *Idiots* may sound strong here, but Wilson makes a good point: only fools rush in to try what's new, novel, or more risqué. He goes on to point out that the real trouble is we're asking the wrong questions. We shouldn't be asking "What can we get away with?" but "What is sex *for*?" While I'm not always one to agree with Wilson, here I think he's right on. So much of Christian talk about sexuality is an adventure in missing the point. We are chasing phantoms.

The way Christians have learned to talk about and think about sexuality has been shaped by a world in which sexuality is one of the few transcendent experiences left. The pursuit of sexual pleasure by any means possible (with a few extreme exceptions) has been given a green light by the world around us because, to them, sex doesn't *mean* anything, doesn't signify anything, doesn't point beyond itself to deeper and more powerful truths.

Only in a world where sex is meaningless does it make sense to use the principles of video games to enable hook-ups (like Tinder). Only in a world where sex is meaningless does sexting make sense. Only in a world where sex is meaningless does it make sense to use images of a nearly-naked woman to sell cheeseburgers. Sex is disposable in this world because *we* are disposable.

In such an empty world, it makes sense that pornography would take a profound hold. Pornography, like all sexual experiences, taps into both spiritual longings and spiritual experiences but does so in a way that short-circuits the body's wiring. It is sex divorced from relationships, sex divorced from affection, sex divorced from commitment of any kind. It provides a fast lane to the brain's most primitive pleasure centers, offering just enough of a corrupted hit of what we long for to sustain our addictions.

While Christians may not agree to this way of thinking about sex, they nonetheless swim in these waters, and these attitudes get absorbed by osmosis. The aforementioned book, with its lists of what's in and what's out and its recommendations (including one for—I swear I'm not making this up—prostate massage) is the product of a pornified culture—a world whose vision of sexuality is primarily shaped by pornography.

When you peel back the layers of conversations that make up the way that Christians talk about sex, you discover a culture that is desperately trying to keep up with all the fun the world around us is supposedly having. But when you pay attention to that world, you find divorce, disappointment, and malaise. Hooking up is fun in the same way that using pornography is; it's a fleeting and ultimately disappointing kind of fun. Sexuality becomes an exchange commodity, not a gift, and that transformation has destroyed the possibility of intimacy and real transcendence.

Christians often lament a culture of sex without commitment. I don't disagree with those critiques, but I would add that just as troubling is a culture of sex without attention. Whether we're talking about hook-up culture, pornography, or the mechanistic attitudes about sex advocated in some corners of the church, we find an attitude that is primarily about pleasure-seeking. One can float through life in the shallows, never really knowing or being known by another person.

Seen in light of the creation story, sex is like the high-church liturgy of a marriage. When the church celebrates the Lord's Supper, each member consumes the bread and wine, remembering that they share in Christ's body and blood. For that moment, something spiritual is made visible as each member of the body shares a common meal and a common cup. A genuine oneness happens at the communion table.

When a married couple unites, it punctuates their covenant in almost exactly the same way. Their two bodies become one flesh, and a spiritual reality is made visible. In an ideal world, this isn't the deepest knowing they share but rather a visible expression of the deep knowing that marks their entire relationship. Their life together, a thousand stories of heartache and laughter, is not overshadowed by sex but punctuated by it. Sex is the "sign and seal" of their covenant, their intimacy, and their oneness.

What is remarkable about the Song of Solomon is not the quality or quantity of their orgasms, but the quality of attention they pay to one another. Sex is a celebration of knowing, a feast of attention, a time when what is cherished about the beloved is celebrated by the lover, and vice versa.

Too often, we not only settle for less, but we devote ourselves to the serious pursuit of less. It's as if someone discovered a love of food and then devoted themselves to the study of Arby's. What we desire is so much more than mere physical satisfaction. It comes only when we learn to live a life of attentive and loving presence.

In her novel *The Goldfinch*, Donna Tartt asks, "Isn't the whole point of things—beautiful things—that they connect you to some larger beauty?"[19]

When we talk about feasts of attention—whether it's an actual feast, an experience of beauty, or sex—we're talking about beautiful things that connect us to a larger beauty. Each one offers a little bit of satisfaction, but that satisfaction is always temporary. That's how appetites work; they drive our lives in a steady rhythm, sending and returning. A feast of attention sends us out into the world refueled, comforted, and with joy in the provision from the Giver of the feast and with joy at the feast itself, but in time, our appetite returns, and we return, once again, to the table.

These beautiful things point to a larger beauty because no feast can ever fully satisfy us. Our satisfaction is always dependent on the provision of others. No meal leaves us full forever. No art can end our desire for beauty. No sexual experience can obliterate our sexual desires. And nor should they. This dependence—this need to return to the source of our good things—is part of our design. In fact, it's just this dependence that makes a feast a wondrous experience. No one eats when they're full, and as Robert Capon put it, "hunger remains the best sauce."[20] We are sent from the table until hunger draws us back again. Hunger is the grace that keeps us tethered to the gifts of the Giver.

It's tempting to say that one day these appetites will be fully satisfied. Jesus did offer living water with the promise that those who drink it will never thirst again. But we also see the new heavens and the new earth as places where a garden grows and where feasts continue. I suspect that our appetites will be transformed and purified, but I doubt that they'll cease altogether. I don't think the goal of resurrected life is a life of autonomy.

Instead, I suspect that our radical dependence will continue. That God will continue to provide. That life will keep a steady rhythm of sending and returning, punctuated by feasts and wonder. It's a life that we can experience a foretaste of now. If we're paying attention.

There are many ways to talk about cultivating a life of attention. Years ago, my friend and mentor Harold Best encouraged a group of artists I'd gathered to become amateurs—amateur historians, amateur musicians, amateur writers or birdwatchers or anything else. The word *amateur*, he explained, means something like "for the love of." Love something, attend to it, and discover its details and its secrets. "Be curious," Harold said, "and creation will never stop entertaining and fascinating you."

I later saw him put this into practice. We were driving to lunch one day when a train stopped us at a crossing. Before I knew what was happening, Harold jumped out of the passenger seat and walked over to the crossing, leaning on the red and white barrier and grinning ear to ear as the train passed. He came back to the car excited, and for the rest of our drive to lunch, he explained to me how diesel trains work, how much torque they need to get a train moving, and how the diesel actually powers generators for electric motors. He went on and on in loving detail and said, "Isn't it fascinating that God knew that the train would exist before he said one word about light or earth? That he saw the possibility of it when he wrote the laws of thermodynamics and gravity and all the rest?"

For Harold, love of trains invites attention, attention reveals the wonders of creation, and creation calls us to worship. This means that whatever weird and quirky thing you might enjoy is an invitation to explore the mind of God.

FEASTING

An easy way to begin cultivating our attention is to throw a feast. Most of us don't know how to feast these days. We know how to eat, and we know how to eat far more than we need to eat. But we don't know how to feast: how to gather around a table, linger over a meal, cherishing the conversations, flavors, and stories that are shared.

Food has always mattered a lot in my family. Some of my earliest childhood memories are of my grandfather wearing a chef's hat while barbecuing chicken out of an oil drum that he'd converted into his backyard grill in Miami. The Cosper men are cooks, and we take our craft quite seriously.

Cooking, for me, is a feast of attention. I cook because I love food, but more than that, I cook because I love cooking. Cooking returns me to both the earth and the Cosmos, away from a world of abstractions and org charts and grand strategies and back to earthy wonders such as chickens rendered crispy or the wondrous and strange things that happen when a dozen ingredients combine in a curry.

A feast takes this world of love and mystery and extends it outward, compounds it with the fearfully and wonderfully made mysteries that make up our friends and family. There are few things in this world I enjoy more than a good feast shared with friends.

HOW TO THROW A FEAST

First, invite the guests. Make sure they know that this isn't just another meal—this is a feast, and we're going to take time to eat and enjoy one another's company. The best feasts are big feasts, so invite a small crowd. You might share some of the following ground rules in advance.

The Ground Rules of a Feast

1. *Turn off your phones.* I know you haven't eaten a great meal without Instagramming it in a few years, but please, show up ready to be present to the actual human beings you're in the room with. Put your phone on "do not disturb" or, better yet, turn it off and leave it in a car/bedroom/nearby dumpster. (At a gathering recently, the host required a "phone stack," where everyone left their phones in a pile by the door.) Exceptions can be made to accommodate being accessible to a babysitter if you've left your kids at home.

2. *Do* **not** *plan on counting calories, carbs, sugars, or any other nonsense.* Feasts are the exception, not the rule, so come ready to eat. You might consider eating a light lunch in order to balance out the serious caloric intake you will experience with us. Obviously, if you have an allergy or a serious intolerance to food, we will serve and accommodate you, but if you're avoiding carbs this week because Oprah said so, then plan on either breaking your rules or staying home. We'll be following Jesus' advice to Peter, killing and eating all manner of flora and fauna.

3. *The giant bowl of buttered noodles.* Some feasts are kid-free, but most feasts will include kids at the table, or at a nearby table, and on feast night, parents and children declare amnesty on trying new things, eating vegetables, and cleaning plates. As a sign and seal of that amnesty, a giant bowl of buttered noodles will be on the table or at the buffet, along with a bowl of shredded parmesan cheese.[1]

4. *Conversations will be driven by joy.* This is perhaps the most important of the rules. At the feast table, conversations should be driven by what people are joyful about, what interests them, and what's worth celebrating. Obligatory conversation about

jobs, bosses, school, homework, the weather, and other boring topics will be curtailed. So reflect before you come to the table: What can we celebrate with you? What are you thankful for? What has ignited your curiosity lately? What stories do you want to tell? (This is hard for people, and it's the duty of the host to help steer these conversations. Occasionally barking "No Work!" tends to get the job done.)

5. *Plan for abundance.* Plan to cook more food than you need and to serve it slowly (giving time for people to make room for more). Going overboard occasionally is a foretaste of better feasts. (Once, I attended a Sabbath dinner with an Orthodox Jewish family in Jerusalem. They welcomed about twenty of us into their home, packing tables and chairs around their small living room. The sheer quantity of food they served that night was astounding. Every time you thought you were done eating, another course came: the bread, the salad, the matzoh soup, the eggplant and hummus, the fish, then the chicken, then the beef, then more cheese and snacks, then dessert, and then more dessert. The host sang and read Scripture and told stories and prayed, and the night is forever marked in my mind. The Sabbath is a celebration that the week is over, that the work is done, and that God has provided. The feast made that reality tangible.)

6. *Lighten up.* Feasts should be celebrations, not formal dining affairs, so don't go crazy with place settings, don't worry if the house isn't perfectly put together, and don't freak out about the timing of your meals unless you're really, really into that sort of thing. Serve some snacks and welcome people into the kitchen while you finish making the meal. My wife and I will often invite friends over early in the day—three or four o'clock—and we'll cook with them, inviting their help on laying out the snacks and slicing the onions.

7. ***Call attention to the feast.*** There's a fine line here between being pedantic and being celebratory, but help people attend to the feast. If you know a little bit about what's been made, share it. Likewise, call attention to the fact that a good meal is a gift, and acknowledge the presence of God in your midst.

8. ***Feasting is a practice.*** Like fasting, feasting is a habit we're cultivating. We want to get good at throwing a feast not because we want to impress our friends but because we want to learn to savor good things and share joy. So treat this like any other practice or habit you're trying to cultivate. Throw a feast, and reflect on the experience. What went well? What would you do differently? Here, I refer less to the cooking—always a learning curve—and more to the conversations and celebrations.

We've often punctuated our feasts with a light liturgy—praying a Psalm to bless the meal and singing the doxology at the end, before people begin to trickle away. Sometimes, we make a point of lighting candles, as with a Sabbath meal, to signify the beginning of the feast and to remind us of God's presence.

Whatever you do, don't get distracted too much by the details—don't fret a burned roast or a dry chicken or a bad mussel (as bad as that can be). Feasting is a habit you're learning and a way of life. All of our feasts will be a little imperfect, but with practice, we learn to come to the table with joy and gratitude and to leave with a little bit more.

SEVEN

The Monastery
and the Road

There's a stretch of country road I drive a few times a year. It seems as though it were designed to perfectly display all that is Kentucky. Between acres of corn and soybeans are town squares with nineteenth-century courthouses, shops full of antiques, and diners that haven't redecorated since the fifties. There are bourbon distilleries that belch white steam and warehouses where their liquor lies dormant for years in charred oak barrels. Sprawling farmhouses with white split-rail fences and families of horses are just down the road from shacks, trailers, and tobacco barns, where bundles of broad, brown leaves hang upside-down to dry.

Perhaps the most otherworldly sight of all is just outside Bardstown. It's a scene transported through time and space from medieval Europe: the Abbey of Gethsemani, a Trappist monastery with high fences of piled stone, whitewashed walls, and a high bell tower. There, a community of monks lives out their days in work and prayer, making cheese, bourbon-infused fudge, and fruitcakes. Throughout the day, they answer the chime of the bell, halting their work and gathering in the chapel to chant the Psalms. Signs everywhere remind visitors that "silence is spoken here."

It's nothing if not an honest attempt at living in another world.

I first visited the monastery almost twenty years ago, shortly after reading Thomas Merton's spiritual autobiography, *The Seven Storey Mountain*. He lived on two continents, lost both parents while still a child, and felt drawn first to the life of an artist and intellectual and later to Catholicism. He took monastic vows and spent the rest of his life at the Abbey, where he eventually wrote that book and many others. He lamented a society

> whose whole policy is to excite every nerve in the human body and keep it at the highest pitch of artificial tension, to strain every human desire to the limit and to create as many new desires and synthetic passions as possible, in order to cater to them with the products of our factories and printing presses and movie studios and all the rest.[1]

Merton knew something was rotten about modern life, and he knew it decades before the internet, before smartphones, before the twenty-four-hour news cycle.

Merton commented on all the ways our culture had become dehumanizing and destructive. In his writing, he called out consumerism, racism, nationalistic ideologies, secularism, and more. All the while, as his journals reveal, he battled with his own impulses to be part of that world. He once fell in love with a nurse in Louisville while staying at a hospital and carried on an affair with her for some time. He could have left the monastery, but he didn't. He eventually confessed his secret and recommitted himself to a life of chastity, solitude, and silence.

Merton described the motive for becoming a monk as "a deep desire of God that draws a man to seek a totally new way of being in the world."[2] That deep desire is what kept him in the monastery when love, fame, or literary success could have provided a path out. If we believe that life with God is possible in this world, and if we believe *that* life is the one we've always longed for, then it would be worth whatever it cost us to pursue it. Merton's life demonstrates such commitment.

When I visit the monastery, I am captivated by the life of the monks. The bells chime at 3 a.m., and they begin their day. Sometimes, when I stay in one of the guest rooms that overlooks a central courtyard, I'll go to the window and watch the monks walking to the chapel in the twilight. They wear brown and white robes and move like ghosts toward the abbey church, where they'll chant the Psalms for the first of nine times that day. At 5 a.m., when they gather again, I'm usually awake enough to follow them to the church. In the predawn, the light hangs low like a mist, coming only from a few wall sconces and candles. The tall ceilings are hung with shadows. I listen to their chants and remember the line from Psalm 57: "Awake, my glory! Awake, O harp and lyre! I will awake the dawn!"

Before the sun rises, the monks are praying and singing, calling themselves and, like the Psalmist, calling the Cosmos to worship.

During the day, I wander the trails that crisscross the woods and fields across the road, where a random bench or chair appears in the middle of a field and where visitors have left scribbled reminders to pray or to seek God on makeshift signs.

Life here is rhythmic and Godward. The sun awakes you, if not the bells, and when it crawls behind the hill on the Western edge of the monastery property, behind a high statue of a cross, you join the monks for the final chants of the day and disappear into the twilight, alone with God in the silence of the sleeping monastery.

Monasticism takes seriously the notion that the world is perilous and toxic for the soul. Its regularity and rhythms are a way of marking life with signposts that remind you that the world is not merely what appears. There is an invisible kingdom at hand, a world we access through Word and prayer, silence and solitude, feasts and fasts, bread and wine.

Of course, I am not a monk. But I have learned much from monasticism in general and Merton in particular. I have come to understand that the Christian life is truly a life, a "way of being," as Merton said. To experience the richness of life in God's kingdom, we must reorder our lives. We need to see through the shallow promises of our culture, and we need rhythms, signposts, and practices that reorient us to another world.

For much of my life, I didn't see things that way. I thought my struggles with faith, doubt, and sin could be sorted out if I got the right information. There had to be a book or a class or a retreat or a conference that could free me from my staggering, stuttering attempts at faith. I devoured books, Bible studies, sermons-on-tape, conferences, and retreats, but it only led to frustration. I didn't know how to change.

> To experience the richness of life in God's kingdom, we must reorder our lives.

There's a scene in *The Matrix* where Neo is being trained to fight with other humans against their evil robotic overlords. Because he was once a slave to the robots, his body has a jack that can connect his brain directly to a computer. The rebels who liberated him use it to download knowledge directly into his brain. At one point, he awakens from a download and says, "I know . . . Kung Fu." From that moment onward, he's a Kung Fu master.

I think many Christians dream of spiritual growth and transformation along these lines. I know I did. We think, *If we can download the Scriptures and a shelf full of commentaries into our brains, we'll have the tools we need to become saints.* The problem with this idea is also what makes Neo's transformation in *The Matrix* impossible in the real world: the body. If someone had decades of Kung Fu mastery downloaded into their brains in an instant, they'd throw their back out performing their first roundhouse kick. Martial arts don't merely depend on the mind; the body must be trained and prepared as well.

The same goes for any skill or art. One needs more than knowledge to play the guitar. It requires hours of training, cultivating a feel for the instrument up and down the neck, and learning to coordinate hands and ears. Playing with a band is yet another layer of learning—learning to feel the music and find one's place in the rhythms of an ensemble. Much more is happening than the possession of information.

The same is true of sports. On his podcast *Here's the Thing*, Alec Baldwin asked NFL quarterback Andrew Luck what he thinks about when he drops back to throw during a game. "You don't want to think about it," Luck replied. He went on to describe how passing mechanics have to be so deeply ingrained into the body that they are on autopilot during a game. The body not only "knows" how to throw but knows how to read the whole field.[3] It's mind-boggling when you think about it. There are eleven men on each team, each one moving separately and simultaneously. It's as if an entire chess match is played in the blink of an eye, each piece moving at the same time, and the quarterback must read these moves, calculate the other team's vulnerability, and attack it. Notice how long it takes a TV announcer to break down a play after the fact; all of that analysis happens in a few seconds on the field, and if your last name happens to be Luck, Manning, or Brady, your body's ability to calculate all of those moves is right more often than it's wrong.

With any skill or performance, information alone is not enough; it must be translated into know-how in the body. It's true of athletes, musicians, actors, and artists, and it's also true of plumbers, woodworkers, engineers, computer programmers, and hedge fund managers. These skills become ingrained in such a way that after years of practice, one can do them with very little thought, trusting gut and intuition. That isn't to say that thought doesn't enter into it but rather that it plays a different role. When one first starts playing the piano, it demands a lot of conscious thought. Ten years later, thinking occurs on a different level. It's a check on the action, or it's used to assess the work. A depth of knowledge is assembled that allows the individual to think at a higher level while the embodied knowledge handles the performance. To put it a little differently, intellectual knowledge has been worked into the body in such a way that the actions a craft requires become second nature, automatic, reflexive. The body is *primed* to do the work because practice has enabled it.[4]

Practice opens up a world. Music becomes a language to people who master the required skills. Without them, you might enjoy music, but you will find that musical expression—music as language that can be translated through an instrument into sounds—is either extremely limited or dead to you altogether. Likewise, if you haven't conditioned yourself with the skills of an NFL quarterback, then you certainly don't want to find yourself taking the snap in an NFL game. That world will be dead to you too. (And you might soon be dead as well. Your body hasn't learned how to live in that world.)

Just as an athlete's body is conditioned and primed through practice to know a skill or discipline, so also are all of our bodies conditioned and primed to know the world in certain ways. Any approach to spiritual transformation that doesn't take this kind of embodied knowledge seriously is bound to fail. Your daily routine

Your daily routine has a worldview.

has a worldview. It orients your body to the world and primes you to experience it in specific ways.

Annie Dillard once wrote, "How we spend our days is, of course, how we spend our lives. What we do with this hour, and that one, is what we are doing."[5] Each moment of our days—our meals, our conversations with friends, our escapes, obsessions, romances, and distractions—is what we make of our lives. Our habits and rhythms of life are formative not only of who we are but how we know the world, including whether we know it to be a place where God is present or absent.

To come to live in the kingdom of God, or to seek to live in a world other than our disenchanted milieu, requires a wholesale reordering of our habits and commitments. As Merton said, once we find ourselves hungering for God, we will seek a whole new way of being in the world.

This depends on a miracle. Jesus said that to see the kingdom one must be born again (Jn 3:3). Rebirth can't be manipulated or forced. "The wind blows where it wishes, and you hear its sound, but you do not know where it comes from or where it goes. So it is with everyone who is born of the Spirit" (Jn 3:8). Living in another world begins when the Spirit whispers life to a dead soul. It's less like being convinced of something and more like falling in love. Once desire awakens, the soul knows a hunger that nothing else will satisfy. Jesus described it like this:

> The kingdom of heaven is like treasure hidden in a field, which a man found and covered up. Then in his joy he goes and sells all that he has and buys that field.
>
> Again, the kingdom of heaven is like a merchant in search of fine pearls, who, on finding one pearl of great value, went and sold all that he has and bought it. (Mt 13:44-46)

The characters in these parables look as though they've lost their minds to the world around them. But they're only doing what lovers do in their wedding vows when they declare they're "forsaking all others." To behold the kingdom of God is to fall in love, and people do crazy things for love. They cross oceans, slay dragons, abandon crowns and comforts. To love is to be willing to die.

In the parables, there's also a concept of hiddenness. The pearl merchant finds the pearl—it doesn't simply fall in his lap. Likewise, the treasure is described as hidden in a field. The verb that is translated as "hidden" is found in a number of spots in the New Testament. For example, Jesus celebrates that the mystery of the kingdom is hidden from wise men and revealed to children (Mt 11:25). It shows up again in Luke's Gospel when Jesus foretells his death and resurrection to the apostles; we're told the apostles didn't understand what Jesus was saying because it was hidden from them (Lk 18:31-34).[6]

The kingdom exists as a world-within-a-world. It's just out of view of ordinary life, accessible not by will or power but by God's grace. The Spirit reveals it to us, and once we see it, we're invited to be one of the crazy ones who give all they have in hopes of living in that hidden world. Paul uses the same word to describe the Christian life: "For you have died, and your life is *hidden* with Christ in God" (Col 3:3). There are layers of hiddenness—the kingdom hidden in a fallen world and our new life hidden with Christ.

How do we live in the kingdom while it remains hidden? How do we devote ourselves in love to another world while this world continues to hum and buzz and grind around us? Seeing the kingdom isn't enough; we must come to *know* it in the same way that an athlete comes to know her sport or an artist learns to paint or dance or sculpt. We don't merely need information. We need to cultivate a way of life that orients us toward that other world. Like the man who found treasure in a field, we need to sell all we have.

Thomas Merton caught that vision. He followed a long tradition of men and women who withdrew from society. In the earliest centuries of the church, Christians ran to the desert. In silence and solitude, they sought God and battled the evil that was both within and without them. Later, some of these desert hermits banded together and formed monasteries.

Monasticism is most certainly an effort to build another world, and I'm not talking about the physical realities of life in a monastery. Instead, I'm talking about the way a monastery intentionally reorders life. What is primary in the monk's life is the chime of the bell, the call to prayer, the church calendar's rhythms of feasting and fasting.

As Merton described it, "The monk seeks to be free from what William Faulkner called 'the same frantic steeplechase toward nothing' which is the essence of 'worldliness' everywhere."[7] It's a way to "protest against the organized and dehumanizing routines of a worldly life built around gain for its own sake."[8] One is drawn to this life by "a deep sense that *God alone suffices*. The need to win the approval of society, to find a recognized place in the world, to achieve a temporal ambition, to 'be somebody,' even in the Church seems to them irrelevant."[9]

The monk lives a rhythm of life that is organized around prayer. God's presence is treated as primary, and the disciplines of a monk's life assume that God is present. The monk lives as if he is certain that God's kingdom is advancing.

And yet, what's troubling about monasticism is its exclusivity. One would hope that any Christian could share the monk's conviction that "God alone suffices." The treasure and the pearl aren't just for monks and nuns. To my mind, there is something cynical in the cloister, perhaps a belief that the kind of communion with God available to the monk is unavailable to the rest of us. A belief that those who marry, have children, run businesses, teach, practice law, or build furniture—that all of us can only hope for second-rate intimacy with God, or second-rate knowledge of that "new way of being in the world."

On this point, I tend to think G. K. Chesterton's famous quip applies: "The problem of Christianity is not that it had been tried and found wanting, but that it had been found difficult and left untried."[10] Perhaps monasticism is a response to the difficulty of Christianity. Perhaps it was assumed that most Christians simply couldn't live that life (or wouldn't try).

This was an important point for the reformers, as Matthew Myers Boulton points out in his book *Life in God*. He says, "These reformers insisted that properly understood, religious disciplines are not rarefied recommendations for cloistered or ordained virtuosos in training. Instead, they are the disciplines of discipleship itself, divinely and apostolically bequeathed to the whole church."[11] The goal of monasticism is too narrow. We shouldn't aim only for "a sacred church alone, then, but rather 'the sacred city.' Not a special spiritual precinct, class of experts, or set of operations, but rather an integral world, in all its variety and ruin, divinely called to both holiness and wholeness."[12]

Calvin dared to believe that the knowledge of the kingdom that was available to the monk was available to everyone.

> If the monk's organizing vocational goal was union with God, so too was the cobbler's. In short, if the whole city was sacred [and not just the monastery], so too was each disciple's whole life. And accordingly, to live into such a life, each and every Christian required this training, this sacred instruction, this program of embodied, regular, formative practice.[13]

Monasticism made

> elite, difficult, and rare what should be ordinary, accessible,
> and common in Christian communities: namely, whole
> human lives formed in and through the church's distinctive
> repertoire of disciplines, from singing psalms to daily prayer
> to communing with Christ at the sacred supper.[14]

Calvin longed for a way of life that allowed every Christian to experience the kind of intimacy with God assumed to be available only
to the privileged few. It would be monastic in that it was intentionally ordered around word, prayer, and community with the saints,
but it would be ordinary in that it could be practiced by anyone. He
rightly understood that our daily, ordinary rhythms of life need to
be reordered. One must, at least metaphorically, sell all one has.

Around the same time I read Merton's *The Seven Storey Mountain*,
I read another book that, in a similar way, changed my life: Jack
Kerouac's *On the Road*.

I've always been struck by what these books share. Both are auto-
biographies featuring young men who aspired to be writers, and both
men longed for a life of depth and meaning. Both attended Columbia
University in New York City. Both books were written shortly after
World War II, and both reflect the spiritual questions of that time.
Both men had compassion for the world and a deep love of humanity.
Most importantly, they shared a conviction that following the cur-
rents of culture wouldn't lead them to a meaningful, wonder-filled life.

And yet, they couldn't possibly be more different. Kerouac and
Merton lived like polar opposites, the one a Bohemian wanderer
who experimented with drugs and sex, the other a Cistercian monk,
theologian, and moral philosopher. While reading Merton felt like

an invitation inward, reading Kerouac felt like an invitation outward, an invitation to notice the beauty of tattered landscapes, the goodness and soul-satisfying power of a simple meal shared with friends and strangers, the transcendent moments that occur in the seemingly mundane moments of everyday life. Merton made me want to seek God in silence; Jack made me want to seek him in the world.

Traveling on a cross-country highway, Jack wrote: "As we crossed the Colorado-Utah border I saw God in the sky in the form of huge gold sunburning clouds above the desert that seemed to point a finger at me and say, 'Pass here and go on, you're on the road to heaven.'"[15]

Everyone Kerouac met along the way might have been an angel or a saint: the girl slicing pie in a diner, migrant workers picking grapes, or even drunk bums sleeping in train cars. His writing is so attentive to the moment, so *present*. To Jack, ordinary experiences and everyday moments are potentially wonderful, if we'll only notice them. And yet, he's also keenly aware of life's tragic sense—an overarching sadness that colors our days.

At one moment in *On the Road*, he's reflecting on the snapshots we take of one another and writes,

> I realized these were all the snapshots which our children would look at someday with wonder, thinking their parents had lived smooth, well-ordered lives and got up in the morning to walk proudly on the sidewalks of life, never dreaming the raggedy madness and riot of our actual lives, our actual night, the hell of it, the senseless emptiness.[16]

Kerouac saw that every good moment is fleeting. Like the author of Ecclesiastes says, life is *hevel*—a breath, a vapor, or smoke. "What is that feeling," Jack wrote, "when you're driving away from people and they recede on the plain till you see their specks dispersing?—it's the too-huge world vaulting us, and it's good-bye. But we lean forward to the next crazy venture beneath the skies."[17]

Reading *On the Road* made me want to love the world, to see it and experience it in all of its diverse and earthy glory and sadness. But it wasn't hard to see that Jack's "way" in the world had a downside. He was seduced by much of the world's darkness and suffered its consequences.

Yet, strange as it might sound, I think Merton and Kerouac were after the same thing. They both had a sense that life was tragic but sacred, that every moment was pregnant with the potential for transcendence. They abandoned a status-quo life and devoted themselves to that search.

I believe that if we want to live in another world, to live in the kingdom of God, it will look a little bit like *The Seven Storey Mountain* and a little bit like *On the Road*. It demands a certain kind of withdrawal, an anchoring in life-orienting habits, rhythms, and disciplines. But it also demands a certain kind of spontaneity, attention to the moment, and a commitment to being present to God and to others, wherever our journeys lead us.

These visions aren't opposed; they're complementary. At its best, the disciplined life prepares us to be open to the world—to spontaneous joy, encounters with beauty, and encounters with

> At its best, the disciplined life prepares us to be open to the world—to spontaneous joy, encounters with beauty, and encounters with tragedy.

tragedy. Likewise, a life that's open to the world can deepen our disciplines, enriching our prayers, bringing the joys and sorrows of life with us as we seek God's face.

What if it's true? What if God's presence is as available to us in our ordinary, humdrum lives as it is to the saintliest saints? What if God is there when we're at our desks at work, when we're chopping onions or changing diapers, when we're lying awake, frustrated and anxious in the darkest hours of the night?

What if God upholds every moment of our lives by the power of his word? What if he were living and active and gifting us with our next meal—be it a Pop Tart or a pot of chili or a pot-au-feu? What if he weeps with us when we weep and rejoices when we rejoice? What if we could connect with God in each of these moments? What if—more than our desires for power, love, sex, and success—what if *he* is what we have been longing for and looking for all of our lives?

To live as if this were true requires more than good ideas and more than mere knowledge. Like Kerouac, it demands attentiveness to each moment. Like Merton, it demands a reordered way of life.

We cannot live in the kingdom of God and leave our way of life untouched. We are too vulnerable to the life-shaping habits of a disenchanted world. We are too deeply formed and oriented *away* from God. This is not to say that God will abandon us—his grace is a gift, and it will not be withdrawn. But it *is* to say that we're missing out.

In contrast, life oriented around the spiritual disciplines is not a pathway to pleasing God but a pathway to experiencing the joy of God that is already ours in Jesus. The disciplines reshape our awareness and perception, and that awareness has a way of growing roots and branches, expanding far beyond our "prayer time" and into our whole lives.

In the Christian life, there are no shortcuts. There is no way to fast track our growth, no jack in our heads through which we can download information and suddenly become saints. There is only the slow and patient work of showing up, reordering our days, seeking God in word and prayer, and looking for him with a moment-to-moment awareness.

This will undoubtedly make us look strange. Like I said, people do crazy things for love. They sell all they have to buy a field or a pearl. They risk marginalization, suffering, and death. They spend hours with ancient texts and whispered prayers. They get caught up by beauty and light, tragedy and darkness. They become marginalized or mocked, and people say they've lost their minds.

But the truth is our strange lives are shaped by a secret—one announced by Jesus with the words, "The kingdom of God is here."

To believe that announcement places us at a similar crossroads to one Kerouac experienced in his own life: "I realized either I was crazy, or the world was crazy," Jack wrote. "I picked on the world. And of course, I was right."[18]

PATHWAY 7
THE RULE OF LIFE

I'm captivated by John Calvin's vision for the City. I'd love to live where the monastic way of life can be expanded to include everyone. Calvin's vision is a bit idealistic (to say the least) and seems even more idealistic in a culture where Christians make up a minority of the population, but the general idea remains appealing. Can we, like those in a cloister, shape our days around work and prayer, making regular contact with God's kingdom along the way?

Life in the monastery is governed by a "Rule of Life"—a set of commitments that frame the monks' days, marking them with habits and practices that orient the entire community to the kingdom of God. For those of us outside the monastery, we need similar guidance. We need a way of framing our days that the disciplines we've been discussing can fit into. We need our own rule of life.

Throughout this book, I've been describing the experience of faith in a disenchanted age—the ways it feels resisted from without and within. I think understanding the spiritual background of our lives and the ways we've already been shaped (for better or for worse) helps us to have more clarity about our spiritual experience. Along the way, I've described disciplines as pathways that might lead us down the road that Jeremiah calls "the good way" and "the ancient path."

My hope has been that these descriptions of where we are and how we've been shaped are comforting to you. I know that reading others—like Charles Taylor, James K. A. Smith, and David Foster Wallace—has been comforting to me. They've helped me understand my own experience of faith, and particularly, they've helped me understand the resistance I've felt. Most of all, they've comforted me with the realization that I am not alone.

Likewise, I hope that the pathways in this book have felt like invitations and that you've seen the way prayer, Scripture meditation, or a good meal can be an intersection between the ordinary and the transcendent. Hopefully, you're a little less skeptical of your own faith and a little more curious about how God may be at work in your everyday life.

If our culture is the background for our spiritual formation, and if the disciplines are pathways, then the rule of life is a roadmap that ties it all together. At its most basic, a rule of life is a plan for growth. What steps are we going to take to reorient our days to God's kingdom among us?

The concept of a rule of life is quite old and has an interesting history (monastic orders developed them in part because of unrest and conflict among desert hermits). What I describe below is a very simple approach to the subject, merely a starting point.[1] Some people use the idea of a rule of life to encompass every aspect of their lives—their relationships, their vocation, their finances, and more. I want to start much more simply. I encourage you to allow the concept to take shape in whatever way makes the most sense to you.

WRITING A RULE OF LIFE

Let's return to the concentric circles described in pathway one. Consider your life divided in years, weeks, days, and hours.

Hours. We'll start with hours, and we'll start by acknowledging that most of us are not prepared for constant awareness of God's presence (like Brother Lawrence) or a minute-by-minute remembering of God (like the missionary Frank Laubach). But it's good to have a few resources available at a moment's notice. These could be breath prayers or Scripture verses you've memorized. You might benefit from having something written on an index card in your pocket or in an app on your phone. (There are many good Bible memory apps—I'm fond of Desiring God's Fighter Verses app.)

The point is to have a plan for what to do in a moment of stress, crisis, or even a moment of rest. If we don't have any available resources in our memory—prayers, verses, and so on—then we're drawing from an empty well. So to prepare for our hours, it's wise to dedicate something to memory. Even if it's just the Jesus Prayer: "Lord Jesus Christ, Son of David, have mercy on me, a sinner."

Days. Our daily routines may be the most crucial place we attend to in our rules, and it's what is most likely to change over time. If you're starting from zero—wanting to begin building new habits from the ground up—I would encourage you to start with beginnings and endings: What are the bookends of your days? For most of us, they're frenzied. Up too late, awake earlier than we'd like, and harried all the way in between.

But God gives sleep to those he loves (Ps 127), and a frenzied life is not demonstrative of great faith. We have good reasons to sleep and sleep well; our lives are in God's hands.

Everyone is different, but I always encourage you to try waking early and going to bed early. If you can rise before the world and start your day in solitude with God, you've already won half the battle; you've remembered God at all. As Woody Allen famously said, 80 percent of success is just showing up, and showing up to meet God in the morning, tired, groggy, half-incoherent, is better than delaying for a "better" hour and not showing up at all.

Likewise, how we end our days matters as well. Most of us crash into bed exhausted, minds rattled from stress, television, and other stimuli, and give little thought to how we might sleep. Here again, showing up at all—acknowledging that you're in the presence of God as you go to bed—is better than nothing.

Beyond these bookends, I encourage you to consider milestones throughout your day. These include transitions from home to work or work to home, mealtimes, and recreation times. The point is not to turn each of these moments into a worship service but to use them as signposts that remind you that God is present. Praying for a blessing over a meal may seem rote or foolish but only in a disenchanted world. In a Cosmos, it's the least you can do to acknowledge the Giver before enjoying the gift.

Beyond this, there are a thousand variations. I'd encourage you to reflect on the various pathways discussed here and ask yourself, how might God be inviting me to take the next step? Don't be a hero; just take a small step that you can stick with—adding one practice at a time. Many Christians take on too much at once, get discouraged in their practice, and end up abandoning all efforts at a disciplined life. If you've established a good morning routine, then consider adding a time of prayer to refocus in the middle or at the end of your day or perhaps on your way home from work. If you've never had a fasting practice, consider that. If you're not giving generously, consider taking a small step there.

If you have a grand vision of who you want to become, there's nothing wrong with writing that out. But implement it slowly. Add one or two practices in simple steps—things you can accomplish in a few minutes or on certain days—and once they're established as habits, expand them or add more.

Weeks and years. In pathway one, I talked about how weekly and yearly habits—like gathering with the church for worship and accountability or celebrating Advent, Christmas, Lent, and Easter—provide a big-picture way of immersing ourselves in the kingdom of God. This subject, like the rule of life, could be explored in much more detail than I have space for here. But at the very least, let me suggest that these outer rings on your concentric circles are integral to a Christian life and should have a central place in your rule. Gathered worship in particular serves as the most visible moment each week of God's kingdom among us.

MY RULE

With all that in mind, here's my rule. It's generally held up as my goal for several years, and you'll see a few moments where there is some variation. It's aspirational; I very rarely hit every point on here in a given week, much less a year, but it's a frame that makes sense and has, frankly, preserved my sanity.

One quick explanatory note—I'm a big fan of prayer guides, and my morning, midday, and evening prayers usually are guided by *The Book of Common Worship, Daily Prayer* from John Knox Press. These prayers don't substitute for my own words, but like the rule itself, they provide some architecture for them.

Hourly

- Breath prayers—Romans 8:1, Colossians 3:3, the Jesus Prayer, and a few lines from scattered hymns.

Daily

- Morning routine—about 45 minutes. I count this as the most important time of the day.

    - Wake between 5:00 and 5:30 a.m.

    - Prayer—including the Psalm of the day and the Lord's Prayer

    - Scripture reading—I rotate between a yearly plan like a Chronological Bible or Robert Murray McCheyne's method or a much less rigorous plan moving more slowly through the Gospels or the New Testament.

– Journaling—I practice "morning pages," which comes from Julia Cameron's fascinating and helpful book *The Artist's Way* (New York: Putnam, 1992). This isn't about keeping a diary of your life's events; it's more like a pressure release valve, allowing you to dump fear, doubt, and anxious thoughts on the page.

– Scripture meditation—End the morning by sitting quietly and reflecting on a single passage for five to ten minutes.

– This may seem like a lot, but each item takes only five to ten minutes. At most, the Scripture readings require fifteen minutes. For me, it's worth the extra time in the morning to set a trajectory for my whole day.

- Midday

  – Guided prayer—five minutes or so, sometime between 10:30 a.m. and 12:00 p.m.

  – Prayer of Examen—about twenty minutes, sometime between 4:00 and 6:00 p.m.

  – I rarely do both, if ever. Which one happens is dependent on what makes sense in the schedule.

- Family Dinner—At least five nights a week, we try to gather around the dinner table and share a meal without TV, phones, or other distractions.

- Evening Prayer—five minutes, right before bed.

Weekly

- Gather for worship with my church.

- Give proportionally from my income.

- Meet with one of two to three friends for check-ins on accountability, marriage, and life. This includes very specific and very personal questions about sin, character, and the pursuit of God.
- Fast one day, about every other week.
- Practice Sabbath

    - In Jewish tradition, the day begins at sundown—and so Sabbath (Saturday) is welcomed with a feast on Friday night. In our home, we observe Sunday as our day of rest, and we welcome it on Saturday night with a regular feast. We make dinner a little bit nicer than other nights, adding an extra course or a dessert. We light candles, take our time, and reflect on both the week behind us and the week ahead. The meal begins with the reading of a psalm and ends with the doxology.

    - As an anchor point in our week, it's been a real blessing, preparing us to gather with the church on Sunday. We don't get to do it every week, and we certainly don't treat it as law, but it's definitely taken on the feel of a family tradition.

Annually

- Observe the Christian year—especially the fasts and feasts associated with Advent, Christmas, Lent, and Easter.
- Take at least a twenty-four-hour silent retreat (either in a cabin, alone, or at a retreat center or monastery) for prayer and self-reflection. This isn't for life planning or career planning but for silence with God.
- Rest with my family by taking a real vacation at least once a year—no social media, no work.

I also consider diet, exercise, and sleep as part of my spiritual discipline routine. This isn't because I think there's direct communion with God available through limiting empty carbohydrates or doing burpees but rather because these practices care for the body in such a way that we won't be kept from practicing other disciplines. If we're always tired from lack of sleep, crashing from a poor diet, or are generally sore, weak, and out of shape, our stamina for prayer, silence, or fasting is going to be weak.

FINAL THOUGHTS

Your rule will eventually look like your life. The "morning pages" practice came about after a series of events in my life made it feel necessary. I didn't include it above, but cooking meals is a bit of a spiritual discipline for me as well. A friend of mine who's a poet writes a poem a day as part of his routine. Another, a photographer, makes a weekly pilgrimage around his neighborhood—the same block for twenty-plus years—looking for something new to see, a new angle, a new object. He counts this as part of his rule of life. For both of these friends, their practice ties their vocation to their spiritual life.

Don't confuse accomplishing what you've developed as your rule with making God happy with you. God is delighted in you long before you get your act together. Ask yourself simply, what do I sense the Lord is inviting me to as I reflect on the season ahead? There is *good* in a life of obedience, in a life that is more and more tethered to God's Word and immersed in God's kingdom.

The goal here is less about goals and more about ways. Your rule is an architecture, a clockworks by which you shape your days. To return to what Annie Dillard said, "How we spend our days is, of course, how we spend our lives. What we do with this hour, and that one, is what we are doing."[2] Your rule is a way of making some decisions, well in advance, of what to do with this hour and that one. Sometimes it will be a grind. Other times it will be sheer joy. Always, it will be worthwhile as you take steps seeking to live in another world.

Epilogue

ONE FINAL WONDER

Lately I've been struck by the image of Jacob wrestling with an angel. The story is in Genesis 32. Jacob is sojourning—which for him typically meant some combination of spiritual wandering and running for his life. One evening, after he sent his entourage across a river,

> Jacob was left alone. And a man wrestled with him until the breaking of the day. When the man saw that he did not prevail against Jacob, he touched his hip socket, and Jacob's hip was put out of joint as he wrestled with him. Then he said, "Let me go, for the day has broken." But Jacob said, "I will not let you go unless you bless me." And he said to him, "What is your name?" And he said, "Jacob." Then he said, "Your name shall no longer be called Jacob, but Israel, for you have striven with God and with men, and have prevailed." Then Jacob asked him, "Please tell me your name." But he said, "Why is it that you ask my name?" And there he blessed him. So Jacob called the name of the place Peniel, saying, "For I have seen God face to face, and yet my life has been delivered." The sun rose upon him as he passed Penuel, limping because of his hip. (Gen 32:24-31)

Commentators differ on exactly what was happening in that moment. Was it an angel? Was it God? Was it some other kind of manifestation? Was it a "Christophany," an early appearance of Jesus? Some even want to spiritualize the wrestling—maybe Jacob dreamed the whole thing and the wrestling was a spiritual battle. This interpretation conjures images of Jacob the mystic, sitting in a lotus position while wrestling God in a dream world. To me, though, that sounds more like a character from *Kung Fu Panda* and less like the brawling, hard-drinking womanizer from the book of Genesis. I imagine the scene more like a bar fight than a spiritual epiphany: Jacob the brute, one of the violent ones that Jesus describes as taking the kingdom by force.

I've tried to imagine this scene—a dying fire casting long shadows on goatskin tents and cold desert sand, feet making sizzling sounds as they slide and scrape, ankles and calves and forearms slick with sweat, stuck with dust, breaths heaving, low grunts, muscles flexed, blood pumping, the body stressed to its physical limits. The story says they wrestled all night. Jacob was desperate: "I won't let go until you bless me." There's a crazed, unrelenting energy to the story.

The craziest thing about Jacob's all-night battle with God is that he *won*. Or at least, he got what he asked for. "I won't let go until you bless me," he said, and God blessed him.

But he also walked away with a limp. To know God and to wrestle with God means bearing the scars of battle. I'm convinced there's no other option. We find rest in Jesus on the other the side of struggles with angels and demons, including those that sow the subtle doubts of disenchantment. It's tempting to hold our struggles for faith up against the struggles of previous generations—Roman executioners and lions and totalitarian states—and to shame ourselves for our weakness. If they could stand off against *death* and believe, why can't I hold off these doubts?

The answer, I believe, is that disenchantment is still the work of principalities and powers. Just like the murdering regimes that persecuted Christians in the past, at its core, a secular world wants to devalue life, enshrine power, and dethrone the Creator God who made the Cosmos and called it good. Our lives may not be in immediate danger—and by no means do I take that for granted—but our souls are as imperiled as ever.

About twenty years ago, a mentor handed me Richard Foster's *A Celebration of Discipline* and that book changed my life. Soon after that I found Dallas Willard, Thomas Merton, Henri Nouwen, and many others. These saints showed me a path through a dark world, and they faithfully accounted for their own struggles along the way.

Unfortunately, they are the exception and not the rule. Many pastors and writers paint a picture of the Christian life that is much more akin to a Thomas Kinkaid painting: everything bathed in amber light, flowers blooming even in the snow, everything peaceful and picturesque. Practice the spiritual disciplines *correctly*, get enough Bible and prayer and silence and solitude in your life, and you can handle anything.

I've come to distrust anyone selling that vision. Reading about the lives of saints, I don't see immovable giants. Instead, I see Merton falling in love with a nurse and having an affair. I see Brennan Manning fighting a life-long battle with alcohol abuse. I see Charles Spurgeon and Martin Lloyd Jones—two of the greatest preachers in the English language—fighting lifelong battles with depression. But Merton came home to the monastery, Manning died declaring "all is grace," and Spurgeon and Jones kept preaching the gospel.

In the Scriptures, I see Peter denying Jesus, showing favoritism against the Gentiles, and being rebuked by Paul. I see David and

Bathsheba. Moses and the rock. Noah and his vineyards. And I see the love that would not let them go.

I mention this because I want to end with one final wonder, one final mystery, and that's the paradox that exists between grace and struggle. The life we want in Christ is ours free, a gift of grace. And yet, experiencing that life on this side of eternity is a struggle.

My goal in this book was to lift the veil a little bit on how the world has shaped us, how we've learned to see things through the lenses of disenchantment. I believe there is a better life available to us and that we can discover a better world when we enter God's kingdom: a world that is enchanted, a world that offers a deeper comfort to the soul and makes more sense of how the world is. But I do not want to make the mistake of saying that living in that world is easy. It's not. But it is the good way. And it's the way of grace.

Somehow, grace abounds in a world full of sorrows. Grace overflows. The more I live and the more I look for it, the more I see it filling the corners of our world. God is a lover, and he's constantly at work chasing his beloved back home. When we begin to pay attention, when Spirit-transformed imaginations look for grace in the world around us, we see it everywhere.

The alternatives to a grace-shaped life are legion: life lived to please the mob around us, life lived to please ourselves, or a life spent so deeply distracted and numb that we please no one and feel as little as possible. These pathways have their own rewards, I suppose, but they leave us feeling empty and unsatisfied. They cannot bring us home. Home comes when we rest in Jesus. And yet, resting in Jesus might require an all-night (or, better yet, a life-long) brawl. Strangely, if Jacob is our model, it's somehow a fight we can win. We grab hold of God and scream that we're not letting go until we're blessed. When that blessing *does* come, it comes with a scar. Or more precisely, a limp.

Does it sound confusing yet? Does it sound absurd? Rest comes with struggle? Blessing comes with wounds? Grace comes from the death of an innocent man?

Then you're getting the picture. Life with God is an invitation into a world where most of what makes sense to you crumbles. It's far richer than you imagined, far less orderly and sensible, and far more mysterious. Like Job, once you begin to see the wonder of it, you find yourself awestruck and, somehow, satisfied.

Grace is easy. Life is hard. So follow Jesus if you must, seek the face of God if you must, but don't be surprised if, after a while, it feels like you've been battling angels in the darkness. Seeking God's face in a fallen world is not the easy life; it's the good life, and a good life is always a life of worthwhile stories and worthwhile struggles.

Acknowledgments

T hanks to the many friends who prayed for and encouraged me as I wrote. There are too many to name.

Thanks to Mike Frazier, Dan Dumas, and Randy Stinson for your hospitality. You provided space and solitude that were essential.

Thanks to Sara Galyon for helping me clean the manuscript up.

Thanks to Don Gates, David Zimmerman, Cindy Bunch, and Helen Lee for believing in and shaping the direction of the book.

Thanks to James K. A. Smith for helping me better understand the world, myself, and all that's shaped us.

Thanks to David Dark, who most certainly lives in a Cosmos and who gave me *The Gift*. Much of this wouldn't exist had you not switched on that particular bulb in my world.

Thanks to Kevin Jamison, Jonah Sage, Trevin Wax, and Daniel Montgomery for reading various drafts and offering feedback.

Special thanks to Dave Harrity and Scott Slucher for relentless encouragement, for talking me off the edge of the cliff more than once, and for taking my Twitter password away (Dave) so that I would finish.

Thanks to Harold Best for being the brightest mind, most honest critic, and most generous soul I know.

Most of all, thanks to Sarah, Dorothy, and Maggie Cosper for interrupting and not-interrupting, for letting me read passages out loud, for letting me write, and for making our home a warm and loving place. Sarah, I love you more than I could ever say.

This book was fueled by Quills Coffee (thanks, Nathan), the music of Dan Phelps, Joe Henry, Elbow, Bill Laurance, and weirdly enough, in the final stretch, by Kanye West and Kendrick Lamar.

Notes

INTRODUCTION

[1] Susanna Clarke, *Jonathan Strange and Mr. Norrell* (New York: Bloomsbury, 2004), 3.

[2] Charles Taylor, *A Secular Age* (Cambridge: Harvard University, 2007), Joseph Bottum, *An Anxious Age* (New York: Image, 2014), and Christopher Lasch, *A Culture of Narcissism* (New York, Norton, 1991), respectively.

1 DISCOVERING OUR DISENCHANTMENT

[1] David Foster Wallace, "This Is Water" (commencement speech, Kenyon College, Gambier, OH, May 21, 2005).

[2] Taylor actually got the term from Max Weber in *The Sociology of Religion*, but Taylor innovated the term in turning it around, describing the premodern orientation toward the world as "enchanted"—a term I'll be using as well. See also James K. A. Smith's *How (Not) to Be Secular: Reading Charles Taylor* (Grand Rapids: Eerdmans, 2014) for a readable and thorough introduction and summary of Taylor's massive work *A Secular Age* (Cambridge: Harvard University Press, 2007).

[3] Taylor, *A Secular Age*.

[4] Louis CK on Conan, "The Fast and the Bi-Curious," TBS, September 19, 2013.

[5] Taylor, *A Secular Age*, 29.

[6] Hannah Arendt, *The Human Condition* (Chicago: University of Chicago Press, 1958), 256.

[7] Arendt unpacks this in a section of *The Human Condition* called "The Discovery of the Archimedean Point," 257-68.

[8] Smith, *How (Not) to Be Secular*, 72.

[9] Robert Ferrar Capon, *Hunting the Divine Fox* (New York: Seabury Press, 1974), 20-21.

[10] Helen MacDonald, *H Is for Hawk* (New York: Jonathan Cape, 2014), 148.

2 MODERN RELIGIOUS SACRIFICES AND THE GOD WHO ENDS RELIGION

[1] David Foster Wallace, *Infinite Jest* (New York: Little, Brown and Company, 1996), 147.

[2] Ibid.

[3] Jason Gilbert, "FaceTime Facelift: The Plastic Surgery Procedure for iPhone Users Who Don't Like How They Look on FaceTime," *Huffington Post*, February 27, 2012, www.huffingtonpost.com/2012/02/24/facetime -facelift-plastic-surgery-for-iphone-users_n_1300496.html.

[4] Charles Taylor, *A Secular Age* (Cambridge: Harvard University Press, 2007), 483.

[5] James K. A. Smith, *How (Not) to Be Secular: Reading Charles Taylor* (Grand Rapids: Eerdmans, 2014), 86.

[6] Matthew Myer Boulton, *God Against Religion: Rethinking Christian Theology Through Worship* (Grand Rapids: Eerdmans, 2008), 71.

[7] Ibid.

[8] Ibid., 73.

[9] Ibid., 74.

[10] Robert Farrar Capon, *Kingdom, Grace, Judgment: Paradox, Outrage, and Vindication in the Parables of Jesus* (Grand Rapids: Eerdmans, 2002), 252-53.

PATHWAY TWO: EXPERIENCING GRACE

[1] Jerry Bridges, *Respectable Sins* (Colorado Springs: NavPress, 2007), 37-38.

3 SELFIE STICKS, SPECTACLES, AND SEPULCHERS

[1] Martin Wendell Jones wrote a great story about his time visiting Bethel for *Christianity Today*. www.christianitytoday.com/ct/2016/may/cover-story -inside-popular-controversial-bethel-church.html.

PATHWAY THREE: BRINGING SCRIPTURE TO LIFE

[1] Joan Chittister, quoted in Oliver Burkeman, "Can You Learn Life Lessons from Monks and Nuns?," *Guardian*, May 8, 2015, www.theguardian.com /lifeandstyle/2015/may/08/lessons-in-time-management-oliver-burkeman.

[2]Donald Whitney, "Praying Through Scripture," http://storage.cloversites .com/compasschurch/documents/Praying Through the Scripture.pdf.

4 SOLITUDE AND SECRECY

[1]"Louis C.K. on Taking Pictures with Fans," *Inside Comedy: Season 2*, www .youtube.com/watch?v=zNoKqhEYfIo.

[2]Hannah Arendt, *The Human Condition* (Chicago: University of Chicago Press, 1988), 71.

[3]See, for instance, this article on the limited capacity of the brain to make decisions, and remember, Jesus had and used a brain. "Do You Suffer from Decision Fatigue?," *New York Times Magazine*, August 21, 2011, www .nytimes.com/2011/08/21/magazine/do-you-suffer-from-decision-fatigue .html.

[4]Hannah Arendt, *Responsibility and Judgment* (New York: Schocken, 2009), 12.
[5]Ibid., 16.

[6]C. S. Lewis, *The Weight of Glory* (San Francisco: Harper, 2001), 45.

5 ABUNDANCE AND SCARCITY

[1]Lewis Hyde, *The Gift: Creativity and the Artist in the Modern World* (New York: Vintage, 2007), 6.

[2]Dallas Willard, *The Divine Conspiracy: Rediscovering Our Hidden Life in God* (San Francisco: HarperCollins, 1998), 63.

[3]Hyde, *The Gift*, 9.

[4]For a brilliant exegesis of desire, advertising, and "the good life," see James K. A. Smith's *Desiring the Kingdom* (Grand Rapids: Baker Academic, 2009). Smith describes the experience of going to a shopping mall where the displays are windows into the good life and sales clerks are like acolytes. We see something we desire, go in, make our exchange, and leave with hopes that this new sweater will satisfy us (pp. 19-24).

[5]David Foster Wallace, *The Pale King* (New York: Little, Brown & Company, 2011), 267.

[6]Slovoj Žižek, quoted in *The Pervert's Guide to Ideology*, dir. Sophie Fiennes (Zeitgeist Films, 2013), DVD. All grammatical errors are original.
[7]Ibid.

[8]In fact, as you may be aware, drinking Coke doesn't satisfy thirst. It's loaded with salt and thus makes us only thirstier.

6 FEASTS OF ATTENTION

[1] David Foster Wallace, *The Pale King* (New York: Little, Brown & Company, 2011), 85.

[2] G. K. Chesterton, *Orthodoxy* (San Francisco: Ignatius Press, 1995), 108.

[3] Simone Weil, *Simone Weil: An Anthology* (New York: Grove Press, 1986), 212.

[4] Robert Capon, *The Supper of the Lamb: A Culinary Reflection* (New York: Modern Library, 2002), 19.

[5] Ibid.

[6] Ibid.

[7] G.K. Chesterton, *Introduction to the Book of Job*, The American Chesterton Society, www.chesterton.org/introduction-to-job, accessed November 24th, 2016.

[8] Slavoj Žižek, "God Without the Sacred: The Book of Job, the First Critique of Ideology" (lecture, New York Public Library, November 9, 2010), www.nypl.org/audiovideo/slavoj-zizekgod-without-sacred-book-job-first-critique-ideology.

[9] Chesterton, *Introduction to the Book of Job*.

[10] Harold Best, *Unceasing Worship* (Downers Grove, IL: InterVarsity Press, 2003), 59.

[11] Chesterton, *Orthodoxy* (Chicago: Harold Shaw Publishers, 1996), 13.

[12] This distinction—between cynicism and skepticism—was pointed out by Penn Jillette in an interview hosted by Alec Baldwin on the podcast *Here's the Thing*. "Penn Jillette's Marathon Life in Magic," *Here's the Thing*, August 18, 2015, www.wnyc.org/story/htt-penn-jillette.

[13] David Foster Wallace, "E Unibus Pluram: Television and U. S. Fiction," in *A Supposedly Fun Thing I'll Never Do Again* (New York: Back Bay Books, 1998), 64.

[14] Hannah Arendt, *Between Past and Future* (New York: Penguin Classics, 2006), 205-6.

[15] Ibid., 206.

[16] See www.soylent.com/about.

[17] Margaret Somerville, "'Healthism' and a Healthy Society: A Conversation with Margaret Somerville, Part II," interview by James K. A. Smith, *Comment Magazine*, September 1, 2015, www.cardus.ca/comment/article/4677/-healthism-and-a-healthy-society-a-conversation-with-margaret-somerville-part-ii.

[18] Douglas Wilson, "Sexual Obedience Outside Scripture," *Blog & Mablog*, January 14, 2012, https://dougwils.com/books/sexual-obedience-outside -scripture.html.

[19] Donna Tartt, *The Goldfinch* (New York: Little, Brown, 2013), 757.

[20] Capon, *Supper of the Lamb*, 115.

PATHWAY SIX: THROWING A FEAST

[1] A note to parents: The joy you take in making and enjoying the rest of the food will, in time, lure them over to the other side. But for now, don't worry about it.

7 THE MONASTERY AND THE ROAD

[1] Thomas Merton, *The Seven Storey Mountain: Fiftieth-Anniversary Edition* (Boston: Houghton Mifflin Harcourt, 1998), 48.

[2] Thomas Merton, *Contemplation in a World of Action* (Garden City: Doubleday, 1971), 25.

[3] Andrew Luck, interview by Alec Baldwin, *Here's the Thing*, March 18, 2013, www.wnyc.org/story/276075-andrew-luck.

[4] For a great book that goes into detail about this kind of embodied knowing, see Joshua Waitzkin's *The Art of Learning*. Waitzkin was the chess prodigy who inspired the film *Searching for Bobby Fisher*, and he went on to be a world-class martial arts champion. The book is half memoir and half how-to, describing a method of learning that Waitzkin argues can lead to mastery in any field. Waitzkin now coaches professional athletes, hedge fund managers, and other elite competitors on his method of learning. For a more academic take on the topic from a Christian perspective, see James K. A. Smith's *Imagining the Kingdom*.

[5] Annie Dillard, *The Writing Life* (New York: Harper Perennial, 1998), 14.

[6] Robert Farrar Capon, *The Parables of the Kingdom* (Grand Rapids: Zondervan, 1985), 134-35.

[7] Merton, *Contemplation in a World of Action*, 9.

[8] Ibid., 17.

[9] Ibid., 24.

[10] G. K. Chesterton, *What's Wrong with the World* (San Francisco: Ignatius Press, 1994), 61.

[11] Matthew Myer Boulton, *Life in God: John Calvin, Practical Formation, and the Future of Protestant Theology* (Grand Rapids: Eerdmans, 2011), 48.

[12] Ibid., 41.

[13] Ibid., 69-71.

[14] Ibid., 121-22.

[15] Jack Kerouac, *On the Road* (New York: Penguin Books, 1999), 171.

[16] Ibid., 241.

[17] Ibid., 146.

[18] Jack Kerouac, *The Vanity of Duluoz* (New York: Penguin Books, 1994), 88.

PATHWAY SEVEN: THE RULE OF LIFE

[1] If you want to study more on the topic, I highly recommend Stephen Macchia's *Crafting a Rule of Life* (Downers Grove, IL: InterVarsity Press, 2012) and Joan Chittister's *Wisdom Distilled from the Daily: Living the Rule of St. Benedict Today* (New York: HarperCollins, 1990).

[2] Annie Dillard, *The Writing Life* (New York: Harper Perennial, 1998), 14.